LOUISE
CONAN DOYLE
MYSTERY #1

Brimstone

JOHN
ALLEN

2018

Brimstone: Louise Conan Doyle Mystery #1

Published by Allen & Allen Semiotics, Inc.
Long Beach, California
United States of America
© 2018

ISBN: 978-0-9842716-9-6

This work is a work of fiction.
Historical characters, events, and locations are used fictitiously.
Any resemblance to actual persons, living or dead, events, or
locales are coincidental.

Cover art by Dean Williams
Cover design and book interior format by redbat design

Other books by John Allen
    Shadow Woman: The Real Creator of Sherlock Holmes
    The Skeptical Juror and the Trial of Byron Case
    The Skeptical Juror and the Trial of Cory Maye
    The Skeptical Juror and the Trial of Cameron Todd Willingham
    Inferno

Watch for
    Gambit: Louise Conan Doyle Mystery #2

dedicated to the memory of

Genevieve Marie Lohrke MacFarland
1935 – 2017

Mother, mother-in-law, friend
Sarcastic, courageous, and loving

table of contents

Chapter one
A SHOOTING ON TORQUAY TERRACE

Having finished raping his wife, Lieutenant William Perenna left the bedroom. Anna Perenna pulled her knickers up from her ankles and attempted to smooth down the back of her dress. She examined herself in the mirror. Other than the tears streaming down her face, she appeared stoic enough. She wiped at the tears with her fingertips, dipped a washcloth in the basin on top of the commode, wrung the washcloth nearly dry, then used it to clean her face.

Suddenly she wrenched off her torn dress, her chemise, and her knickers, tossing each piece of clothing to the floor. Then, leaning with one hand on the commode, she scrubbed her entire body harshly, taking care only when washing her swollen belly. She dried her body, then gingerly cleansed her privates twice, grimacing in disgust as she did so. She donned clean undergarments and her other dress. *My only dress*, she thought, as she pulled it over herself, intending nevermore to wear the other.

Standing again in front of the commode, she used the mirror to examine her hair. She was not surprised to find it hopelessly disheveled. She used several pins to return it to a semblance of its original arrangement.

She walked directly from the bedroom to the kitchen, such being the arrangement of their strange little house. She filled the teakettle and placed it on the stove, leaving it to heat as she walked through a short passageway to the front room. There she faced her husband, just that day returned from Afghanistan, again fully in uniform, absent only his boots. He stood there, bitterly angry, an open locket in his hand. He screamed at her about the shame she had brought upon him, and he hurled the locket at her. She caught it, trapping it with both hands against her dress. After making sure the photograph inside was undamaged, she closed the locket and held it to her bosom.

She stood there, defiant, wondering that she had ever been afraid of him, feeling new anger and hatred, her resolve building, ready to boil over. *Never again*, she decided. *Never again.*

FRIDAY MORNING, 14 MARCH 1879
TORQUAY TERRACE
CLIFTON, ENGLAND

A gunshot!

The short and sharp report threw Louise into a sprint. She broke step with her brother, lifted up her skirts and petticoats, and ran toward the sound. John grasped at her, missed, and yelled after her to stop.

She did not analyze how or why she identified the sound as a gunshot, but there was no doubt in her mind as to its cause. Three steps into her headlong dash, cautionary impulses rose to compete against the rush of excitement that propelled her.

She had not, of course, anticipated hearing such an extraordinary sound on such an ordinary neighborhood morning. The sound seemed particularly ominous and sinister, though, and nearby, seeming to come from a house up the road, on the right, the fourth or fifth house, perhaps the sixth. Her boot heels sounded against the cobblestones as she ran between two-story brick houses on either side. Unsure what she might do when she discovered the gunshot's location, she pressed forward against a rapidly growing sense of foreboding.

As she approached the fourth house on the right, the front door slammed open, a woman stepped out and peered further up the street, a look of alarm on her face and a damp dishcloth in her hands. Louise passed her without stopping, intent now on the sixth house. It captured her attention, being so different from the others, an ancient single-storied cottage covered in sooty plaster, a small-paned, heavily curtained window on the far side of its front door, dying flowers in a cracked pot under the window adding to the aura of age and neglect.

Though disadvantaged by her short legs, her crinoline, and the corset restricting her breathing, Louise covered the ground with surprising agility. When nearly within arm's reach of the door, her right foot rolled off a jutting cobblestone and she went hard to the rough surface. She took the brunt of the fall on her right arm, stones tearing through her coat, dress sleeve, and first two layers of skin, scraping her cheek and temple. Her ankle screamed for her to stay put. She managed nonetheless to regain her feet and hobble the remaining distance. John was, by then, only a few steps behind her.

The door was unlocked, as indicated by the knob's willingness to turn, but it refused to open. After several hard shoves, Louise realized that the door was as unusual as the rest of the house, designed to open outward. As she pulled it open, she detected lingering white smoke, a faint smell of charcoal, and a nearly imperceptible taste of brimstone. In a far room, a teakettle began to shriek, a timely accompaniment to the gruesome scene before her. A cold wash of shock halted her in the doorway. She did not hear John's gasp at her shoulder as they both stood frozen.

Near the center of the small room before her, standing in profile, was a young woman, her face sunk into her hands, her tearful sobbing interrupted only by plaintive pleas for forgiveness. She was domestically disheveled, and her auburn hair was disarranged. She was conspicuously pregnant.

"Oh God, oh God, oh God. What have I done?" she moaned. "Forgive me, forgive me, please, dear God, forgive me. Oh God, oh God."

On the floor, about four feet from her toes, pointing away from her, lay a revolver. Louise followed its aim to the left.

Not far beyond the muzzle were the unshod feet of a young, well-proportioned soldier, nearly supine, his head drastically angled against the wall. Even as Louise watched, a rivulet of blood leaked from the wound in his forehead, flowing past blank, staring eyes, running alongside his nose, dripping off the side of his chin, and staining the right shoulder of his rumpled uniform. Nearly six feet above his head, a gory scarlet burst marked the wall, with elongated drops of blood and gobbets of brain matter spattering the tattered wallpaper and the cheap, ornately framed mirror that hung there. What might have been a bullet hole was centered in the splotch. Below that, a smear of blood led down the wall, ending somewhere behind the dead man's head.

Louise found her eyes drawn to his face. She gulped and forced herself to take in the scene carefully, still horrified by the gruesome details. Youthful, tanned skin covered the soldier's rectangular face. Brown eyes stared across the room, as best they could, one being fully opened, the other half-closed. A trim mustache extended on either side of his Roman nose, just above a pair of thin lips suddenly rendered pale.

Beneath the prominent chin buried in his chest was the uniform of an Army officer. The long, dark blue coat bore the brass insignia of a second lieutenant on its narrow collar; six brass buttons, each properly fastened to the top, but no other decorations, not even on the sleeves or shoulders; no ribbons on his chest, no sash over his shoulder, no sword and scabbard at his hip—merely a broad belt worn high on the waist, with an empty holster. The coat covered the waistline of his khaki trousers, just as the trousers covered most of the crisp new socks on his bootless feet.

Louise surmised the handgun on the floor was the officer's service revolver, recently trained on its owner and victim. It seemed such a small item to be responsible for extinguishing a youthful life.

Four feet back from the revolver were the worn, brown shoes of the sobbing woman. She was clad in a plain brown muslin dress straining to cover her swollen belly and breasts. Its only decorations were the teardrops that fell past the hand she used to cover her face. Her other hand protectively cradled her belly, inspiring a rush of empathy in Louise.

"Oh God, oh God. Forgive me, dear God, forgive me," the woman repeated, and swayed where she stood, suddenly on the verge of falling. Louise moved to steady her, but Louise's sprained ankle pronounced itself seriously injured. She would have fallen had John not grasped and steadied her.

The sobbing woman suddenly quieted, though the tears still flowed. She had become aware of Louise's presence. Turning towards her, she used her right hand to smooth her ragged dress, to no effect, and thereby exposed a dirty, tear-streaked face and watery eyes filled with shock and bewilderment. "Please forgive me," she said to Louise quietly, with a vague sweeping motion of her right hand, seeming to assume responsibility for everything—the state of her attire, the condition of the room, and the body lying against the wall.

"I'm fine," Louise assured John, grasping the doorframe and balancing on her left foot. "Steady her."

John released his sister, stepped forward, and put his arm around the weeping woman, escorting her to a worn divan to the right of the door. As he did so, she begged him also for forgiveness, and then wilted onto the seat.

Louise hopped to the divan and sat beside the gravid woman, cradling the woman with her undamaged left arm, brushing curls of tangled hair away from the woman's tear-streaked face with her scraped and sore right hand. "Shh, shh," Louise whispered. "God will forgive you. Lean on me. Let me hold you. Let the tears flow onto my shoulder. God will forgive you. He forgives the truly repentant."

John stood observing his sister comforting the taller and much larger woman, concern and kindness shining from Louise's round, sweet face. Louise soothed the widow using her dainty hands, and she murmured quiet reassurances, as individual strands of Louise's mussed brown locks mingled with the tangled auburn hair of the sobbing woman.

Automatically, subliminally, Louise began to take in the details of the nearly barren room. On the wall to Louise's left were the blood-spattered mirror and the grisly stain. On the wall opposite the divan hung a poor, undersized reproduction of a blacksmith working a horseshoe beneath a large tree. Next to the print teetered a rickety cabinet, doors open, revealing a few books and puny keepsakes, the most prominent being a framed photograph of the young lieutenant, stern and proud in his uniform, unmarred by the nastiness that awaited him.

Beside the cabinet, directly across from the divan, was a passageway into the back of the house, whence the kettle screamed intolerably. John disappeared through the passageway and, a few moments later, the sound of the kettle wavered and quieted.

Along the wall just to Louise's right was a small parlor stove. Despite the chill outside, the stove was idle, its firewood bucket empty. The unseen kitchen stove was apparently being used for both cooking and space heating. The front room was accordingly cold and uncomfortable.

It was into this unwelcoming room that two men noisily burst, burdened with a bewildering assortment of field view cameras and gangly tripods. They quickly assessed the situation and began setting up their tripods and attaching the cameras to them. The taller of the two prepared to photograph the body, the shorter to photograph Louise and her pregnant charge. The taller of them lifted a cramped wire cage holding a large and belligerent black cat. He examined the creature's pupils, and shouted, "Expose for fifteen seconds." The cat hissed in return and growled when the cage was set back on the floor.

Events seemed to slow and happen simultaneously. Police rattles sounded outside; a gathering crowd of neighbors, drawn by the shot, raised objections to being pushed aside; the cat yowled; the photographers pulled black hoods over their heads and opened their lenses, one pointing at the body, the other at the pregnant woman, who cried out and buried herself further into Louise's shoulder. Louise tried to use her tiny body to shield the woman, to little avail. The smaller photographer urged both women not to move, not to spoil his exposure. The taller one had no similar problem with the corpse.

John appeared from the kitchen corridor, made a quick appraisal, and yelled, "Leave her be!" shoving the shorter photographer from beneath the camera's black hood. Aroused by this invasion of the prerogatives of the fourth estate, the shorter photographer pushed back, and the two slightly built men grappled each other clumsily to the floor, toppling the camera in the process, and kicking the revolver beneath the divan.

John was slightly larger than his opponent, but consumptive. His *Mycobacterium tuberculosis* took a bit more of him each day, thereby negating any size advantage. The two men tussled about until, from seemingly out of nowhere, an unfeasibly large constable appeared and lifted them each by the collar, handing them in midair to his junior partner, who had entered on the gigantic constable's heels. The larger constable bellowed, "Put 'em in the Black Maria, when it arrives."

In the hands of the smaller constable, the two squabblers returned to their own feet but remained in the grasp of the law. Louise opened her mouth to protest but thought better. John wasn't harmed, and he was now safe from the pugilistic photographer.

"My camera!" cried the photographer, as he and John were hustled outside.

"The cameras are evidence," said the commanding constable, flatly. "You can have them back after the trial."

The second photographer, whose camera had all the while been taking an exposure of the body, decided he had no time to spare. Working as quickly and quietly as possible, he replaced the lens cover, removed the partially exposed plate, secreted it in his coat, and scampered from the room, camera and cat in hand, his efforts at stealth somewhat thwarted by the yowls of the protesting cat.

The room became suddenly quiet and intimate with only four occupants remaining: Louise and her distraught charge, the prodigious constable, and the young Army lieutenant with a bullet hole in his forehead. The constable considered his limited options and addressed Louise.

"Tell me about it," he insisted, presuming substantial authority. Louise paused to precisely order the events she was tasked with reporting.

"I heard a gunshot. I ran in. He was dead, there; she was

standing, there," replied Louise, pointing to the center of the room, "sobbing."

"Then you weren't directly involved?"

She shook her head as the enormity of the situation began to come clearer to her. The constable eyed her skeptically, homing in on her mussed hair, disheveled state, torn clothing, and bloody face.

"I fell while running here," she volunteered, divining his thoughts.

"Where's the gun?" he asked, looking about the room.

"Underneath," she said, nodding downward. "It got knocked there during the row that you broke up."

"We'll talk about that," he said, kneeling to look under the divan.

Two constables entered, one of them the junior constable who had transported John and the unknown photographer. "Black Maria's on its way, sir," said that one. "Collins will put them two inside. I made sure they was shackled."

"There's a gun underneath," stated the senior constable, pointing to the divan. "Retrieve it."

"Yes, sir," replied the subordinate. "Excuse me, ma'am," he said to the inconsolable woman, hoping that she would move her feet. When she failed to do so, he tried repeating himself to Louise.

"I've injured my ankle," Louise answered quietly, "and I'm supporting a grieving woman. I would appreciate it if you could manage without me having to resettle."

"Of course." He blushed.

Removing his helmet, he lay flat on the floor and, from the side of the divan, managed just barely to reach the revolver. He dragged it from beneath the divan, stood almost at attention before his senior constable, and presented the weapon. He then recovered his helmet, installed it smartly on his head, and stiffened to await further orders.

The senior constable sniffed the revolver, examined the cylinder, and counted the chambers still showing bullets.

"You saw this weapon when you came in?" he asked Louise.

"Yes."

"Where was it?"

"On the floor, as I said, a bit to your right."

"And where was she?"

"Close to where you are standing now, a bit further back."

"So the gun was at her feet?"

"Not quite. She was facing the wall. The revolver was a bit in front of her, approximately four feet, I should say."

"Was there anyone else in the room, other than Lieutenant and Mrs. Perenna?"

"I don't know them by name."

"The woman in your arms, Miss, is Anna Perenna. That—" the senior constable said, pointing to the body, "—was her husband, William Perenna. Until very recently, he was, for the last year, faithfully serving Her Majesty abroad. I was unaware until just now that he had returned to England."

"God forgive me," Anna murmured.

"Now," asked the constable firmly, "was there anyone else in the room when you arrived?"

"No," said Louise.

"And your name?"

"Miss Louise Hawkins."

"How is it that you came to be the first to enter after the shooting?"

"I was walking with my brother, John. He was one of those two men in the scuffle. We were six houses away when we heard the gunshot."

"In my experience," said the constable warily, "a young woman, such as yourself, does not run towards a gunshot."

Not detecting a question, Louise sat silently, her attention on the constable, a weary smile on her lips. The constable scowled, as he realized no response was forthcoming. "Where do you live?"

"We have rooms at the Montrose Boarding House."

"On Regina Square?"

"Indeed."

"I thought that was for ladies only."

"They make exceptions."

"How is it that I have yet to see you around?"

"I have only recently returned from Switzerland. We're staying here for the air. My brother's consumptive."

"One of the two I picked from the ground?"

"Yes."

"What was that about?"

"The photographer was going to take a picture of us, of me holding this woman, comforting her. John took exception."

"Please forgive me," Anna pleaded yet again.

"She's been saying that frequently," observed the constable. "Was she saying it when you entered the room?"

"Yes."

"That will be all. A detective will be contacting you and your brother for interviews. You will probably be called to testify at the inquest. You're free to go."

"I'll wait here with Mrs. Perenna."

"We'll take care of her," said the constable, his voice darkening. "You will leave. A crime has taken place here, and you have already made a mess of the scene."

"I can't."

"You can't what?"

"I can't leave."

"Why is that?"

"I'm injured. I've twisted my ankle. I don't think I can stand on it."

"Constable," the senior officer said without looking away from Louise, "you will assist Miss Hawkins to her room at the Montrose. Release her brother and have him help you."

———— ✦ ————

Friday midday, 14 March 1879
Montrose Boarding House, Regina Square
Clifton, England

Sixty-year-old widow Elizabeth Croton idled in her most comfortable chair, sipped tea, picked up her tatting from the side table, looked out over her tidy front garden, and monitored her domain beyond. Because she had placed her chair within the cozy space created by her lovely bay window, and because she faced that chair outward, she could view the entirety of Regina Square. Her tenants were working, walking, or passing their time quietly in their rooms. The breakfast dishes were tidied away, and tea was something to be fretted over later. For the moment, she could partake of the view, speculate on the lives of the young couples meeting in the park, and pass judgment on the apparel and habits of neighbors strolling by.

She noticed a Clarence cab coming up Merchants Road. What interesting story might it hold? Curiosity welled up inside her as the driver reined his horse to a stop directly in front of her boarding house. A jolt of excitement ran through her as John Hawkins jumped from the far door, followed by a young constable. John rushed to the near side of the cab and opened the door. The constable moved more slowly, arriving nonetheless in time to help Louise from the cab. Louise placed an arm around the shoulders of each of the two men, both of whom crouched to accommodate her petite stature. Louise, with their help, hopped on her left leg towards the entry.

The landlady sprang from her chair, bustled out of her room, passed through the entryway to the front doorway, and met Louise and her supporters before they reached the porch. Seeing Louise's torn coat, bloody face and tangled hair, Mrs. Croton slapped her palms to her florid cheeks and exclaimed, "My Lord! What has happened? You poor dear. We must get you fixed up. Let me help you up the steps. No, no, I guess they can manage that. Bring her into my room. She can lie on my sofa. There's no way she can be going up and down two flights of stairs. Oh, my Lord!"

"Thank you Mrs. Croton," Louise responded calmly. "I assure you, I shall heal quickly, and I much prefer the privacy of my own room." She could imagine the fussing that would take place if she acquiesced to her landlady's invitation.

The constable and her brother supported her as she hopped up the front steps and made her way to the foot of the stairs that led to her room. There they paused.

"Whatever has happened to you?" Mrs. Croton persisted.

"We'll speak of it soon, I am confident of that," replied Louise.

Confident, indeed, thought Louise. If Mrs. Croton didn't get satisfaction soon, her curiosity might fair prostrate her. "For now, though, I need to figure out how I might hop up these stairs."

The stairway leading to her room was too narrow for even two people climbing side by side, much less three. Louise would have to manage it on her own. Unfortunately, the wall along the right side of the stairs offered no support, and the rail on the left was ill positioned.

With John and the young constable behind her, she placed her left hand on the rail, rocked back and forth, hopped, and slipped off the first step, tumbling forward, banging her left temple in the process.

Her protectors grasped for her, but to no avail. Though they had been well prepared for her falling backwards, neither had anticipated that she might fall up the stairs.

The landlady *oh-my-lorded*.

Louise lay face down on the steps, taking a few still moments to assess her injuries, commune with her humiliation, and devise a plan to right herself. She took a deep breath, resigning herself to the loss of both independence and dignity.

"Help me roll over, please," she said, "and assist me to Mrs. Croton's sofa."

There was no graceful way of righting her. Through Louise's inelegant efforts and their somewhat indelicate graspings, the two men managed to soon have her sitting on the first step. Mrs. Croton contributed a few more "Oh my Lords" and some ineffectual fluttering about.

"That was simple enough," Louise quipped. "Now for the easy part."

She raised her arms and locked hand to wrist with each of her two flustered assistants who pulled her to her feet, balanced her as she hopped into the landlady's apartment, then eased her into a sitting position on the midnight blue, tufted velvet sofa. Mrs. Croton hastily removed half dozen throw pillows, rearranging those that remained, fluffing them to new heights.

"Lay her down this way," she instructed the men, "so her injuries may be better tended."

"Thank you for your kindness, Mrs. Croton," said Louise.

The young constable helped Louise lie back, and John gently lifted her legs onto the sofa. With her head propped up by a pillow and her legs fully extended, she barely fit between the intricately tatted antimacassars draping each armrest.

"It's a good thing I'm so short," she added, grimacing as she tried to settle comfortably. The lumpy horsehair stuffing of the sofa did not oblige.

John carefully unlaced and opened her right boot as gently as possible, pulling it off with his free hand. Louise suppressed a groan as the others hovered to witness the damage.

Bit by bit, John inched Louise's sock down her calf and off her foot. The ankle was substantially swollen but not yet discolored.

"You lie still, dearie," ordered the landlady. "I'll get something to clean that pretty face of yours. Then we'll fetch a doctor to examine that ankle and that ghastly bump on your head. Well, both bumps."

Louise smiled as best she could. It was a poor effort that went unnoticed by everyone but John. The landlady imperiously beckoned the young constable to follow her to the kitchen.

She's bustling, thought Louise. *This does not bode well.*

"Can I get you anything?" asked John, eager to help. It was a turnaround for him. Usually Louise was John's caretaker. Now she needed him, and he was determined not to let her down.

"Not at the moment, thank you. I suspect, though, that I will soon be wanting something to read. I've been making my way through Tacitus's *Agricola*. Perhaps you could fetch that for me."

John turned and started from the room.

"And the current issue of *English Women's Journal*, please."

John hesitated. "Right." He made to leave again.

"And the *Scientific American* supplement."

John nodded as he strode from the room.

The young constable returned to Louise's side to take his leave. "I hope you will soon be back on your feet, Miss."

"Thank you, constable, both for your assistance and your kind words. I assume you have revealed all to my curious landlady?" Louise dearly hoped so, since it might shorten the cross-examination yet to come.

He smiled, put his fingertips to his helmet, bowed slightly, and departed.

Mrs. Croton returned with a damp cloth and a bottle of Ferris's Carbolic Acid, the word *POISON!* printed large on its label.

"Thank you, Mrs. Croton, but I've been experimenting with antiseptics other than carbolic."

John returned just then, short of breath, and attempted to hand the awkward armful of requested reading material over to his sister, who refused it with a gently upraised hand. He set the book and magazines on a table behind him.

"Thank you, John. I won't be reading just yet. Would you kindly retrieve the cake of Thymol soap from my vanity? For Mrs. Croton, as a gift."

"Same manufacturer as your carbolic," Louise explained to her landlady. "Ferris and Company, down in Bristol, on Union Street. The soap is made of culinary thyme instead of poisonous phenol, and seems to work just as well."

The landlady nodded and, having some experience of Louise, prepared herself for the dithyramb to follow.

"The name *thyme*," Louise continued, "is said to be from the Greek word *thymus*, which means courage. The ancient Egyptians used it in the mummification process. Over the centuries, it has been used as perfume and incense, for preserving food, as a mosquito repellant, and as a treatment for various ailments, from melancholia to vaginal irritation."

"Miss Hawkins!" blurted the scandalized landlady.

"It's also been used as a treatment for tuberculosis and epilepsy. I'm particularly interested in it for those reasons, to test its efficacy."

"We'll get a doctor here to examine your ankle," said Mrs. Croton, in desperate hope of forestalling any further discussion of thyme and its unspeakable medicinal uses.

"I expect there will be no need for that," said Louise confidently. "It's badly sprained, to be sure, but I don't think it's broken. If I keep off it for a few days, I will soon enough be hobbling about."

John returned, winded. He offered the cake of soap to the landlady, who seemed reluctant to touch it.

"Thank you, John," said Louise, holding out her hand. "I believe I'll be washing my own face. Would you bring a basin of water, a washcloth, and a towel?"

John turned just as Louise added, "And a hand mirror, please."

Still panting, he simply nodded his acknowledgement.

"And," Louise admitted, as much to herself as anyone, "I suspect I'll be needing a pair of crutches."

———✦———

Friday evening, 14 March 1879
Montrose Boarding House, Regina Square
Clifton, England

Before the sun set, Bristol Police Detective John Reeves stepped from the hansom cab that stopped in front of the Montrose boarding house. Even before he reached the steps, he was confronted by the stout, flushed, formidable form of Mrs. Croton.

"I'm Detective Reeves, ma'am," he said tipping his hat, "of the Bristol Police. I'm here to interview both Mr. John Hawkins and Miss Louise Hawkins about the murder earlier today on Torquay Terrace."

"He's out to rent a pair of crutches for Miss Hawkins, and she's in no condition to see you right now. You'll have to come back tomorrow or the next day."

"I'm afraid I must insist on seeing her now," said the detective, politely but firmly.

"I'll see him, Mrs. Croton," Louise shouted from within the house. "Please allow him in."

"You're not decent," the landlady argued over her shoulder, "in your nightgown and all." She seemed oblivious to the indelicacy of informing the detective and the neighborhood of Louise's deshabille.

"If Miss Nightingale can bathe an injured soldier in his altogether," Louise joined, with equal volume, "then Detective Reeves should be allowed to interview a witness to a deadly shooting, even if that witness is in her nightgown. Please allow him in. Or shall I hop out there?"

Mrs. Croton harrumphed but stepped aside. The detective suppressed a grin and followed Louise's voice into the landlady's apartment. He found Louise resting on the sofa. He moved a small side chair nearby, seated himself, then fixed Mrs. Croton with his stare.

"I'll be in the kitchen," she said, reluctantly taking the cue, "should you need me."

Louise had washed the blood from her right cheek and temple, but the rasped skin was still obvious, scabbing over. Round bumps had firmly established themselves on each temple; the one on the right being from her tumble outside the Perenna residence, the one on her left a persistent reminder of her stubborn effort to hop upstairs. Her right ankle and foot were wrapped tightly with swaths of gauze bandages, the entire assemblage resting on a pillow.

Reeves turned his attention to her, taking immediate notice not only of her injuries but also of her striking blue-green eyes and the fierce intelligence behind them.

"You are quite a sight, Miss Hawkins," he observed, hoping the remark would be taken to refer only to her injuries. "I'm not sure whether you were brave or foolish for running towards the gunshot, but you are an interesting person in either case."

Louise nodded, assessing him as she did all new acquaintances: tall and fit, but not remarkably so; distinguished instead by his crop of dark curly hair, hooded brown eyes, and by lips that seemed unusually pink. She noted the tacit admonishment in his remarks, and chose to ignore it.

"Constable Murger informed me that I would find you here at the Montrose," he continued, "and that you are new to Clifton."

"I assume Constable Murger is the Goliath of Bristol, that gargantuan constable who insisted I leave the house on Torquay Terrace, rather than comfort Anna Perenna."

Reeves nodded, hiding a quirk of a smile.

"He is incorrect. Both John and I lived in Clifton previously, from '71 to '76. I was a resident pupil at Badminton House, on Worcester Terrace, less than half a mile distant. John was, during the same period, at St. Michael's Hill Street School, slightly more than a mile from here. So we are hardly new to Clifton. The constable did not have all the facts at hand before reaching his conclusion."

"He told me also that you have recently returned from Switzerland. Was he correct in that?"

"Yes. John is in the early stages of consumption. My mother took him to Switzerland for the air, and I was fortunate that they wanted me to join them. As the two youngest of seven children, John and I have always been close. We look after one another."

"Where did you stay while in Switzerland?"

"What does any of this have to do with the shooting on Torquay Terrace?"

"Oh," said the detective, smiling. "My grandfather was French, my grandmother Swiss. They met in the romantic town of Geneva. I was born in the not-so-romantic town of Sheffield, of all places. I've never been to Switzerland myself, so I am interested in your stay there, if my questions are no imposition."

Louise gave him a smile, and he felt its effect.

"I understand," she said. "We stayed mostly in the tiny village of Vernet, on the northeastern shore of Lake Geneva."

"I've never heard of it."

"It's near Montreux, and likely to be swallowed by it soon. We lived there for a year, giving the air and the region's famous grape cure an opportunity to work on John's consumption. He didn't deteriorate while we were there, nor was he cured. So we made our way slowly up the Valley of the Rhône, experimenting along the way with various spas and baths and alleged cures, traveling as far as Zermatt, near the base of the Matterhorn, to study the effects of oxygen deprivation. That experiment was particularly interesting to me, if not helpful for John."

She examined Reeves's face to determine if he was growing bored with her monologue. He seemed interested, so she pressed on.

"We met Mark Twain while we were climbing to Zermatt, and dined with him there. He and his friend Joe Twitchell were hiking through the region, with Mr. Twain writing a book about their adventures as they roved about. I spoke with them well into the night, long after John and Mother had retired, about his impending book, the Shakespeare dispute, and of the Beecher-Tilton controversy. Mr. Twain even offered me one of his cigars. I accepted."

"Miss Hawkins!" the landlady shrieked from the kitchen.

Reeves smiled, quite taken by the mischievous twinkle in the eyes of his subject. Louise briefly examined the ceiling, believing it rude to roll one's eyes, then lowered her gaze and responded to Reeves with a grin of her own. He flushed a bit, and hoped she would not notice.

"The cigar was not nearly so disagreeable as I had anticipated," she continued, "but Mrs. Croton and the rest of decent society insist that I not make a habit of it. Two absolutely charming and fascinating men they are, Messrs. Twain and Twitchell. Our meeting was purely happenstance, but one of my fondest memories."

"You can be certain, then, that I will be on the lookout for Mr. Twain's next book. Perhaps it will tame my frequent thoughts of wayfaring. Or it may merely inflame them. In either case, Miss Hawkins, I thank you for the temporary diversion from the misery and heartbreak that is so common to my work."

"And thank you, Detective Reeves, for the opportunity to take some fond memories out for a stroll. Now, pray tell, how fares Mrs. Perenna?"

"I placed her under arrest, but she refused to speak with me. I understand that she has not spoken with anyone since."

"It's a terrible thing."

"Indeed," agreed the detective.

"I presume you are now prepared to get to the heart of the matter."

"If I may," he said, reluctantly. "How is it that you came to be on Torquay Terrace at the time the pistol was fired?"

"John and I were out for our daily constitutional. We were making our way, in intentionally circuitous fashion, to the suspension bridge, our frequent destination. John faces north along the Avon, and takes deep breaths of whatever sea air finds its way this far inland. I marvel at the engineering that allows a roadway to span such a chasm. Torquay Terrace was simply one of many possible streets between here and there. We had not previously walked it. I opted for it this particular time because I was taken by its name. Elizabeth Barrett Browning, one of my favorite poets, summered in Torquay in the hopes its air would relieve her consumption."

"Do you believe it was an omen?" he asked her.

"No," Louise answered flatly. "Merely another coincidence, of which there have already been untold multitudes, of which there will be infinitely more."

"Where were you when you heard the gunshot?"

"We were walking west along Torquay Terrace, six houses removed."

"Approximately six houses away," echoed the detective, verifying her answer.

"*Precisely* six houses, not counting the one directly to our right at that moment, but including the one in which the shooting took place."

"You know for certain that it was six houses," asked Reeves, "not five or seven?"

"Yes."

"How?"

"I have an inexplicable knack for detail. I routinely notice things that seem quite invisible to others," she hedged, scarcely able to say out loud that she went through life with her eyes open when so many others were blinkered by presumption, assumption, and doggedly willful ignorance.

"Then you would indeed be almost unique," said Reeves. "Most witnesses are terrible at recalling accurate details. Though we all consider ourselves perceptive, few of us actually are. I'm certainly not. In many instances my clear recollections are simply wrong. I suspect we're much more inclined to remember what we wish to believe, rather than what we have actually witnessed."

"You interest me, Detective Reeves."

"As you do me," he replied, with considerable understatement. "Give me an example of your percipience."

"Perhaps, after I quiz you first. How many steps are there ascending to the entryway of this building, not counting the porch itself or the walkway leading up to the steps?"

The detective was first surprised by the simplicity of the question, and then flummoxed by his inability to answer it. He thought of climbing those steps just minutes earlier. He tried to recall which foot he had used first, and which foot he landed on last. "Five," he said, trying to hide his confusion, and failing.

"One of the steps has a chip along its right edge. The chip is approximately three quarters of an inch long. Which step?"

He had no idea but figured he had one chance in five of being correct. "The third."

"There are four steps," said Louise in matter-of-fact fashion. "None of them is missing a chip along the right edge. The second step, however, is missing a chip along its left edge."

"You have been up and down those steps many times," Reeves observed, "giving you the opportunity to view them."

"That makes little difference, I assure you," Louise replied calmly. "In fact, the more frequently one sees something, the less one observes it."

"Then take me as an example. You had not laid eyes on me until minutes ago. Describe some detail about me of which I might be unaware."

"I choose not to."

"Why?"

"Because my observations sometimes give me insight that I feel I should not have. And because it would discomfort you to learn what I now know of you, based solely on observing your mannerisms."

"Surely you jest."

"Not in the least."

"Tell me, then, just one mannerism that you've noticed."

Louise sighed. "Several times you touched your left thumb to the base of your ring finger. You didn't notice yourself doing so, but you realize it now that I've mentioned it. That's why you now look so surprised."

"It's a perfectly innocuous tic, nothing more."

"No, it is not, and you have my sincerest sympathy. I have some sense of how much you must miss her. I fear we will lose John to the same disease, and I suspect I will follow him."

The detective folded his arms across his chest, took a deep breath, and closed his eyes. He sat there for a bit before quietly asking, "How could you know?"

"Early in our conversation, I realized that you were either married or had once been married. Few men speak to a woman with such sincerity without having been married to one whom they have deeply loved and respected. When I was speaking of Switzerland and our search for a cure to save John, I noticed your thumb reach for your ring finger. There is no remaining physical indication of your having worn a ring there, but I have no doubt that you did. When I coupled your once-married state with your reaction to John's consumption, I was all but certain. You hide very well your underlying grief, but it left me with no doubt. As I said, Mr. Reeves, I'm sorry for your loss. I hope that you can someday reconcile yourself to it."

Reeves seemed to yank his attention back to the matter at hand. "You have been summoned to appear at the inquest into the death of William Perenna." He rose and reached into his coat pocket for an official-looking document. He handed it to her, and she accepted it. "I have no doubt you will tell them exactly what you witnessed this morning. I'll not make you tell it here as well as there, but will take your inquest testimony as your police statement. Good day to you, Miss Hawkins. I'm sorry if I have distressed you in any fashion."

He turned and left. Louise calmly watched through the bay window, in hopes of following his exit, but was unable to catch any glimpse of him. Mrs. Croton walked in from the kitchen, drying a plate.

"So you chased away another one," she said to Louise, who wasn't sure if the landlady meant another police officer or another potential suitor. Having thrashed that subject to death on previous occasions, Louise declined to pursue the matter. Instead she opened the summons and read.

> *Summons for a Witness, to wit Louise Hawkins, resident of the Montrose Boarding House in Clifton, a suburb of Bristol, England.*
>
> *Whereas I am credibly informed that you can give evidence on behalf of our Sovereign Lady, the Queen of England, touching on the death of William Perenna, now lying dead in the Dead Room of the Bristol Police Central Station, in the County of the Town of Bristol, I therefore, by virtue of my Office, in Her Majesty's name, do charge and command you personally to be and appear before me at the Full Moon Inn and Tavern, on Broad Street in the Town of Bristol, at two of the clock during the afternoon, on Monday the seventeenth day of March of one thousand eight hundred and seventy-nine, then and there to give evidence and be examined on Her Majesty's behalf, before me and my inquest. Hereof fail not, as you will answer the contrary at your peril.*
>
> *Given under my hand and Seal this fourteenth day of March of one thousand eight hundred and seventy-nine,*
>
> *Quinton Welch, Coroner.*

Louise folded the summons and placed it on the table nearby. She looked again out the bay window, this time with no hope of catching even a glimpse of John Reeves, detective for the Bristol Police Department, a sad and lonely widower yearning for an idyllic life in a place beyond his reach.

chapter two

MR. DAVID LINDSEY

John, weakened by his affliction and weary from the prior day's events, idled with Louise in their landlady's apartment. "How about this one?" he said. "It's from the *Bristol Evening News*: 'Brutal Murder: Pregnant wife shoots husband who had been abroad for a year.'"

As Mrs. Croton cleaned in the kitchen, the siblings compared newspaper headlines.

"Or this one," said Louise, "from the *Evening Star*: 'A Bullet to the Head: Pregnant wife shoots soldier husband when accused of infidelity.'"

"Here's the *Bristol Post-Boy*," said John. "'Promiscuous Wife Murders Hero Husband.'"

"You've collected seven newspapers so far," said Louise, "each of them having a different headline to tell the same story: an unfaithful wife murders her husband. The focus will always be on her infidelity. They will convict her in the press before she ever steps into the dock."

"This one," said John, "the *Bristol Mercury and Universal Intelligencer*, says that neighbors heard screaming and yelling just prior to the shooting. I don't recall any screaming and yelling. Do you?"

"Certainly not," replied Louise. "Just the gunshot, then the boiling kettle, then Anna quietly begging forgiveness."

"This one," said John, "reports that Anna admitted shooting him."

"Not while I was there, she didn't."

"Perhaps they mean afterwards."

"What does it say?"

"It's the *Times and Mirror*. It reads:

> *Soon-to-be Mother Confesses to Murder. Yesterday, in a modest, well-kept Clifton home, a woman seven months pregnant murdered her husband of two years by shooting him in the forehead with his own revolver. Coroner Quinton Welch declared Lt. William Perenna of Gloucestershire's 12th Bombay Infantry dead at his house at 22 Torquay Terrace, not far from the zoological gardens. It was the Lieutenant's first day, perhaps even his first hour, home, after having served honorably in Afghanistan for at least the last year. Apparently distressed by a hurtful argument over her obvious and undeniable infidelity, Mrs. Perenna used Lt. Perenna's own revolver to fire a single bullet into his head. Even before the police arrived, a neighbor discovered the pistol at her feet, the murderess weeping and begging forgiveness for shooting her husband. She was arrested by Bristol Police Detective John Reeves. Coroner Welch intends to hold the inquest no later than Monday next, and it seems certain that the unfaithful wife will be charged with the murder of her brave husband. The question on everyone's mind is: Will she hang while still with child?*

"Well," said Louise, "they don't have to twist it very much to make her seem absolutely guilty. The pistol was not quite at her feet, and she never clarified the sin for which she felt contrite. Perhaps she was begging forgiveness for being unfaithful."

"Regardless," said John, "there's no doubt that she murdered him."

"I'll concede there's *little* doubt," said Louise, reaching for yet another paper. "Still, I'll await more data before reaching a final conclusion. And there is no discussion whatsoever regarding what might have prompted her to—Hello, what's this?"

Louise held aloft an eight-page newspaper, barely noticed among its much thicker competitors. "The *Bristol North Star*. I've never heard of it. From its size, it must be a new operation, apparently the work of the very photographer you so heroically thumped for me yesterday."

"Let me see," said John, rising from his chair to read over his sister's shoulder.

"He writes of it differently than do all the others. More objectively. See? Despite the roughing-up by you and the police."

"Mostly by me," said John, with a grin.

"He was smaller than you," Louise quipped. "You should only rough up people your size or greater."

"Then I should have no one I'd dare to rough up, save the man who wrote this article. How do you know it's our photographer?"

"Because he mentions the photograph that his associate took of the body. Give me a bit of room and I'll read it to you."

The article began:

> *Tragedy on Torquay Terrace! Yesterday at 11:42 in the morning, this editor was wandering among you, seeking to learn and write stories of life in Bristol and its environs. With my associate and camera in tow, I heard a gunshot ring from nearby Torquay Terrace. Rushing to the scene and pressing through the rapidly gathering crowd, I entered a house to find the body of a uniformed officer of Her Majesty's army lying dead against the wall, a gaping bullet wound in his forehead. My associate managed to secure a single photograph of the body while I was assaulted and detained by multiple parties, including Constable Henry Murger of the Bristol Police Department.*

"I detained him first and most forcibly," John cut in, feigning offense of his exclusion from the story. Louise smiled and continued reading.

Though many circumstances of the shooting remain unclear, I can report the following evidence as fact, based on my brief presence and limited observations. Number 22, the house now at the center of the tragedy, is located on the north side of Torquay Terrace, approximately halfway along. Upon entry, I spied the body to my left, a revolver on the floor near his feet, and two women on a couch to my right. One of those women was comforting the other, a distressed woman repeatedly asking for forgiveness, but saying nothing to shed any light on what may have transpired.

"I didn't make even a mention," John sniffed.

"Were you aware of the reporters from the instant they entered?" asked Louise, ignoring his interruption.

"No. Once I could take my eyes off that ghastly sight, I became preoccupied by you and your usual concern for the downtrodden and helpless. Who could be more helpless than a mother-to-be who has just murdered someone? And there you were. Then I went to quiet the teakettle."

"I was barely able to let her go when they pulled me from her," said Louise. "To leave her there, so alone, surrounded by so many imposing figures ready to haul her off, it nearly broke my heart. I can't ignore what she has done, but certainly something horrible must have driven her to it."

"And you are going to try to discover what that was," said John. "I know you. You will not sit idly by while they convict and hang her."

"There's a child involved."

"I suspect they'll wait for the child to arrive before they hang her. I'm unaware of authorities ever knowingly hanging a pregnant woman."

"But some women may have been with child without our knowing. It's simply too sad to think of it so directly. Allow me to finish the article."

The victim was Lt. William Perenna of the Gloucestershire Regiment. He had been abroad for fourteen months, serving Queen and Country in Afghanistan. The woman was his wife, Anna. She is being held at Central Station on Bridewell, and, according to the police, has been silent since being removed from her house. The coroner, Mr Quinton Welch, attended the scene personally, pronouncing the victim dead as of 12:42 p.m. Mr Welch informed me that he has contracted the renowned Dr Daniel Weston to conduct the autopsy, which will take place this day at the Central Station dead room. The single photograph we managed to obtain is too gruesome to be included in these pages, but it is available for viewing, for a halfpenny a peek, at the home office of your North Star, on St. Stephen's Street, directly behind the Post Office on Small Street."

Louise scanned the front page for the editorial information, found none, and turned the page.

"Mr. David Lindsey, publisher and editor. You know, John, he interests me. He provides his paper free to his readers, and then charges them to see a grisly photograph. His paper is thick with crass advertising, but it also includes a list of quotations from Mary Wollstonecraft's *A Vindication of the Rights of Woman.*"

"I've never heard of her."

"She was the mother of Mary Shelley. Perhaps you have heard of *her*?"

"Of course. *Frankenstein.*"

"Very well. Mary Shelley's rather liberal lifestyle seems to be an inheritance from her mother. After two public and ill-fated affairs, one of which led to a daughter out of wedlock, Mary Wollstonecraft married the political philosopher John Goodwin, an early anarchist. Have you heard of *him*?"

"No," admitted John.

"Wollstonecraft died giving birth to the daughter who later became the wife of that brilliant libertine Percy Shelley. The widower Godwin attempted to honor his wife in his memoirs, but the memoirs were far too candid. Mary Wollstonecraft fell into disfavor and her writings have been largely ignored. Now this Lindsey fellow uses an eighth of his tiny newspaper to provide quotations from her work. I particularly like the third, the seventh, and the last."

She handed the paper over her shoulder to her brother. As Mrs. Croton set a tea tray on the small table nearby, John settled back into his chair and read the lines aloud:

> *It is vain to expect virtue from women till they are in some degree independent of men.*

> *Make them free, and they will quickly become wise and virtuous, as men become more so; for the improvement must be mutual, or the injustice which one half of the human race are obliged to submit to, retorting on their oppressors, the virtue of men will be worm-eaten by the insect whom he keeps under his feet.*

> *But what a weak barrier is truth when it stands in the way of an hypothesis!*

"Hear, hear!" interjected Mrs. Croton. "I never realized how much I could accomplish on my own until my dear Wendell passed. May the Lord bless and keep him. Our marriage now seems as if it deprived me of much I might otherwise have accomplished."

"Well said," replied Louise. "I believe I will hop over and visit this Lindsey fellow. John, will you please whistle me up a cab?"

"But you can't even get your boot on, much less laced."

"You have tightly and excessively wrapped my foot, I believe, to immobilize me. It's a bit enlarged and sore, nothing more. And I have the crutches you so generously secured for me."

"If I can't stop you, at least I can escort you."

"Good. It's always nice to have someone to lean on."

SATURDAY MIDDAY, 15 MARCH 1879
OFFICE OF THE *BRISTOL NORTH STAR*, ST. STEPHEN'S STREET
BRISTOL, ENGLAND

The Clarence cab made its way up St. Stephen's, amid other cabs and carts and the routine foot traffic of the bustling city. The offices of both the *Times and Mirror* and the *Evening Times* passed to the right, each presenting itself in ostentatious, well-marked, clean-windowed, and well-staffed fashion. The office of the *North Star*, by contrast, was so unremarkable that Louise and John would have missed it, save for the motley crowd of the avidly curious queued outside. The line was long enough to block the entrances of other businesses.

The cab halted at the curb, and John helped Louise make her exit. Despite her crutches, he refused to let her stand on her own, insisting on carrying her like a bride over the threshold of the *North Star*. She held awkwardly to her crutches, failing to avoid knocking into a few of those clutching their halfpennies, hoping soon to satisfy their salacious curiosity after a long wait.

"Excuse us, please," John said. "We have business inside and the lady cannot stand."

The queue parted, grudgingly. Someone held open the door.

The front office was clear of all furniture, save the single desk and chair of the same young man who, the day before, had whisked the exposed plate and the unhappy cat from the crime scene. Along two walls hung multiple copies of the single, underexposed photograph that he had taken at and from the scene. One or two onlookers stood before each copy, intent on the image, ignoring the scene being played out before the desk. There, a well-dressed gentleman of substantial age and self-importance shook with anger barely contained.

"This is not a fair or a carnival," shouted the outraged gentleman. "This is a street of professional offices, and I will not have mine further disturbed by your cheap stunts and gimmicks. If you do not bring this display to an immediate end, I shall yet again call the police on you yellow dogs and have these people removed."

The gawkers evidenced no concern about being ejected, focusing instead on the photographs. One of them was heard to murmur, "Harlot!" A tweed-suited bachelor remarked to his friend, "I'd let no hussy of mine do that to me."

"I will relay your message to Mr. Lindsey," the employee politely told his antagonist.

"Balderdash!" growled the old businessman, who then stormed from the room, brushing past Louise's wrapped ankle without notice or concern.

"John and Louise Hawkins to see Mr. Lindsey," said John in his most professional voice.

"He is not taking visitors," said the desk-minder without looking up, seemingly writing copy for the paper.

One of the viewers squeezed his way out of the room and was replaced instantly by the next.

"Ha'penny in the coin box, please," chanted the young photographer-turned-receptionist.

"I recognize you from the murder scene," said Louise. "I saw you rush the photographic plate from the room."

The young man's interest was engaged, at least enough to look up from his scribbling and take in the lady whose feet did not touch the floor, and the increasingly strained smile on the face of her bearer.

"I was one of the two women seated on the couch," continued Louise.

"Yes, I remember you now," he said, rising from his chair.

"I was there too," said John.

"That I don't recall, but there was a lot going on."

"Of course," said John.

"And what is your name, kind sir?" asked Louise, in the charmingly modest fashion that she found elicited more answers than did straight-out demands.

"Jeffers, miss. Jim Jeffers, at your service."

"We were impressed by the reporting of the story in your morning edition," she offered. "We would like to compliment Mr. Lindsey on his concise and even-handed reporting style."

"Perhaps she could sit in your chair," John ventured.

"Actually, Miss Hawkins," said Jeffers, "I drafted that story for him."

"I thought as much," she replied with a friendly smile.

The young reporter beamed.

"I'm sure Mr. Lindsey would want to speak with you. You'll find him in back," he said, pointing to a door on the rear wall, "probably setting type."

"That's very kind of you, sir."

Jeffers bowed slightly, then returned to his chair, his writing, and his chant of "Ha'penny in the coin box, please."

As John carried Louise through the door, she was struck by the mechanical majesty of the scene before her. On the far side of the room was the printing press, a bewildering assemblage of cast iron gears, plates, spindles and rotating drums. At one side of the press a powerful and grimy young man turned a large wheel to roll an even larger drum against a plate, one that slid back and forth beneath. Hovering above the press, a graying man stooped on an elevated platform, placing blank sheets of paper, one by one, on the rotating drum. With the rhythmic clanking, each blank sheet was pressed between the drum and the oscillating plate, then dropped onto a growing stack at the far end of the machine, waiting to be collated and folded.

The heady smells of printer's ink and solvent filled the air, and smears of ink covered the hands of the printer's devil and much of the floor.

"Closer, closer," Louise urged her brother.

Near the printing press, John at last relented, lowering her. She placed her weight on her uninjured foot and steadied herself with a hand on his shoulder.

"You're small," said John, massaging his biceps, "but not completely devoid of weight."

Louise didn't hear him. "R. Hoe & Company, New York," she murmured, enthralled, reading the large lettering stamped on the side of the press. "Early model, obviously. Manually driven. Single cylinder, so each double-sided sheet must be fed twice through. No paper roll feed, no mechanical folder, no mechanical collator. Hmm, two seconds for each side, four seconds for both, and each folded sheet creates four newspaper pages. His eight-page newspaper therefore needs two sheets. That's eight seconds on the printer for each copy, seven and a half copies of his little newspaper per minute, four hundred and fifty copies per hour, four thousand and five hundred copies during each ten-hour shift. That assumes, of course, that the stout young man turning the wheel can continue at this pace for an entire shift, or be replaced by someone of similar endurance. Quite remarkable."

She paused to appreciate the machine's steady cadence.

"Can you hear it, John? That's the sound of information and wisdom being given wing. Have you ever thought of it in that sense, Mr. Lindsey?" she asked of the short man behind her.

The stealthy gentleman started, having thought that his presence was unnoticed.

"Ah, I suppose it is poetic," he said, "in a mechanical sense."

Louise turned her head to examine him. He was no more than an atom taller than she, with coffee-colored hair curling at the neck and intelligent gray eyes set beneath a prematurely furrowed brow. He had no facial hair whatsoever, only a blemish of ink on the right side of his chin.

"I suppose an introduction is unnecessary on my part," he said, rounding to face them both. "Nonetheless, I am David Lindsey, owner, publisher, and editor of this modest newspaper. I am glad to make your acquaintance—Miss Louise Hawkins, I presume." He bowed. "And I apologize for thrashing you so soundly yesterday, Mr. John Hawkins," he added with a rakish grin. "I got your names from the constable after my release from the Black Maria."

"I'm glad to find you uninjured, sir," replied John, grasping and shaking the outstretched hand, "after the terrible beating I inflicted upon you."

"So you've seen our antiquated press," said Lindsey. "Allow me to get you one of our caster chairs, Miss Hawkins, and I'll show you about."

From the typesetting area where four employees were hard at work, Lindsey pulled a heavy, rococo-style chair, the cast-iron base of which had four caster wheels, allowing him to roll it toward Louise. It was upholstered in black velvet and seemed entirely too extravagant for the mundane use to which it was being put.

"I see you find this modern chair as interesting as our antiquated press. My typesetters need such movable and comfortable seating if they are to work efficiently for long hours each day. It is actually typesetting, not printing, that limits the output of our little paper. I need one skilled typesetter for an entire shift to prepare a single page. I have two men in my employ with the necessary skills and speed, and five apprentices. I will need twice or thrice that number if I'm to turn out daily editions. Were it not for these chairs, I would need half again that many. Here, give it a try."

Louise lowered herself into the chair. As she leaned back, she was startled that the chair leaned with her, her feet leaving the floor as she tilted.

"That's the usual reaction," said Lindsey, chuckling "for people sitting in it for the first time. You won't fall backwards unless you try very hard to do so. These four pairs of curved supporting bands down here act as springs, you see, allowing the seat to tilt in any direction, and the spring resistance grows as the tilt increases."

"It is unsettling at first," conceded Louise, "but it quickly becomes quite comfortable and natural. Where did you get it?"

"Thomas Warren's American Chair Company, out of New York. Warren calls it his Centripetal Spring Armchair. They're not popular here, though. Unlike our more pragmatic American brethren, English businessmen consider comfortable chairs almost immoral. My competitors prefer rigid seats, to enforce an upright posture, supposedly as a sign of refinement and willpower. I prefer rapid typesetting. It swivels, too."

With her good foot planted on the floor, Louise rotated the chair first to her left, then to her right. Then she pushed herself backwards and laughed in unabashed merriment as the chair rolled across the floorboards.

"I must get one of these," she said.

"I'll be glad to allow use of that one, if you wish to hire on as an apprentice typesetter."

"It's an unusual and generous offer, Mr. Lindsey, but I must decline. I've come here to talk to you about the shooting yesterday."

"Of course. And I'm quite interested in speaking with you as well. Let's sit at that table, there, and we'll talk."

To John's evident discomfort, Lindsey grasped the back of Louise's chair and wheeled her across the room to a large table. The table, piled high with a confusion of papers, was surrounded by six thin-framed and lightly upholstered Trafalgar chairs. Lindsey shoved the papers to one side, removed one of the Trafalgars, rolled Louise into the vacant spot, and took the seat to her left. John sat at her right.

"Thank you each for your kind attention," said Louise. "As you can see, Mr. Lindsey, I managed to injure my ankle amidst all of the excitement yesterday."

"I was aware of your injuries," said Lindsey. "I am, among all my other roles, a reporter at heart. Now, what did you wish to speak of?"

Louise straightened her back and laced her fingers on the tabletop.

"Of all accounts we read, yours was the most restrained. You didn't claim to know what had actually taken place, and you certainly didn't attribute a motive, or pass judgment on whatever affair must have taken place in Lt. Perenna's absence."

"I'm reluctant to conclude a story too far in advance of the facts," replied Lindsey. "I realize that such brazen speculation might increase circulation, and I understand the value of circulation as well as my competitors, but I have, shall we say, loftier goals in mind than simply growing the size of my paper. I must first be true to my principles."

"And those include," asked Louise, "promoting the rights of women?"

"I'm proud of my work, and I certainly make no secret of it. I will write as harshly about a woman's behavior as a man's. However, in this shooting, there are two aspects I find curious enough to give me pause. Have you examined the photograph that I have so tastelessly put on display?"

"No," said John and Louise simultaneously.

"Would you like to?"

"Absolutely," Louise replied quickly, but John's slight intake of breath tempered her enthusiasm. "Assuming, of course, that it will help you make your point."

Lindsey shuffled through the papers to his left. He pulled out copies of the photograph and handed one to Louise, another to John.

"It's terribly underexposed. We were in a bit of a rush. It nonetheless highlights the issues of interest to me."

"Is that why you had the cat," asked Louise, "to determine the exposure time?"

"It's an idea that Jeffers had. You must have met him in the office already. He believes he will be able to determine the correct exposure time from the size of the cat's pupils."

"And how is that experiment going?" asked Louise.

"The cat escaped. Our light-measurement device is once again in pursuit of the lady alley cats of Bristol."

John glanced at his copy of the photograph, raised his eyebrows, and recoiled. Louise focused on her copy.

"Do you notice anything?" asked Lindsey.

"The lieutenant's left hand seems to be smudged. I didn't notice it when I saw him lying on the floor, but I see it clearly now."

"It's not unusual for eyewitness accounts to be incomplete, or even diametrically opposed to fact. Do you notice anything else in the photograph?"

"Everything else seems in accord with what I know about the shooting. I just can't imagine the source of the smudging on his hand."

"Take a close look at the bullet wound itself," Lindsey suggested, narrowing his eyes.

"It's gruesome, to be sure, but I don't know what more to make of it. You must see something in it, though, or you would not have pointed it out."

"It's torn and gaping, not round," Lindsey prompted.

"Surely that's a trifle," said John, "when weighed against the more obvious and easily understood evidence."

"It is the obvious that most often leads us astray," replied Lindsey. "The trifle is what most frequently cautions us against doing so. We ignore trifles at our own risk."

"What do you see that is wrong with this wound?" asked Louise, without moving her gaze from the photograph.

"I've seen more bullet wounds than I care to remember," said Lindsey. "Entrance wounds tend to be tight and round, like the bullets that create them. Exit wounds tend to be larger and misshapen. If this is an entrance wound, why then is it not circular?"

Louise pressed her lips together as she considered the question. After some moments she asked, "Why did you choose not to mention either of these issues, the smudging or the shape of the wound, in your account?"

"I don't yet have an explanation for them. If I mention these oddities prematurely, my competitors may bumble upon a solution before I do, and I will have lost a story that could make the *North Star* famous."

"If this is so important to your newspaper," asked Louise, "why do you share it so freely with us?"

Lindsey smiled. "Reporter's instinct."

"So you intend, somehow, to investigate these issues further?" asked John.

"Yes."

"And how might you do that?" pressed Louise, at last setting her copy of the photograph aside.

"I need to examine the wound and the hand carefully, and obtain clearer photographs of them. I therefore plan on entering the dead room, after midnight tonight, to examine and photograph the body."

Despite the printing press's incessant clanking in the background, Lindsey's words hung more heavily than the thickest silence might have.

"Would you care to come along?" he asked suddenly.

Louise barely managed to suppress a grin.

"You're not seriously considering this nonsense!" exclaimed John. He feared that his sister's curiosity and urge to help the downtrodden were burning any prudence right out of her.

Louise ignored him. "Mr. Lindsey, I might ask what makes you believe that I might be interested in such a thing?"

"There's something different about you," Lindsey replied. "I know of only one other woman who would have run towards that gunshot rather than away from it. You're of a different sort than most, as I am, which makes us alike."

Louise stared at him, her face revealing nothing, intrigued for reasons she did not yet fully understand.

chapter three
THE DEAD ROOM

At 2:58 a.m., two minutes before the time arranged, Lindsey knocked on the heavy steel door at the rear of the Central Station. A charwoman opened the door, accepted the second half of her payment in a work-roughened palm, and then left the four unauthorized visitors to their business. Aided by her crutches, Louise followed Lindsey inside. John and Jeffers brought up the rear. Distributed among the men were two cameras, two tripods, and twenty unexposed photographic plates.

The odor was worse than Lindsey had cautioned. *Perhaps not worse*, thought Louise, as she pressed her handkerchief to her face, *but different.* The dampness of the walls seemed to add weight to the handkerchief. Indeed, all her clothing seemed to suddenly hang more heavily on her shoulders.

Lindsey found and lit one dim lamp, then another, and another. In the growing light, there appeared a row of gray stone slabs at waist height, each tilted slightly forward for drainage through a hole near each foot. A small channel in the stone floor guided unspeakable fluids from each table to a grate near the far wall.

On most of the slabs lay the naked carcass of a man or woman. Their predominant hue in the lamplight was blue-tinted, white flesh devoid of blood. On a few bodies, contusions and bruises showed blue and green, and a putrid yellow. Some darkened toward black.

Some bodies displayed knife wounds; one woman's face was swollen and rigid, her blue tongue protruding between her teeth. A few of the corpses retained a somewhat natural form in the rigidity of death. Others were little more than misshapen assemblages of suppurating meat.

John stood frozen, looking unwell. There was no dignity here, and no comfort for the living or the dead.

"Step outside if you're going to be sick," Lindsey ordered, as he made for one body at the far side of the room.

John quickly dispossessed himself of the photographic kit he carried, sprinted from the dead room, and was soon heard vomiting in the alley. The unflappable Jeffers somehow hoisted the equipment that John had abandoned, adding it to everything he was already carrying, and then joined Lindsey beside the body of William Perenna. There, the two of them began setting up the cameras, one camera directed at the smudged hand and the other at the forehead.

Louise examined the room. Along the back wall hung the lamentable rags, petticoats, and trousers previously worn by the souls so immodestly displayed on the slabs. Ignoring the clicking and clacking of cameras being readied, Louise studied both the clothing and the bodies. She took note of the sound of trickling water, sought its source, and found it above the head of each body: small nozzles releasing light sprays of water.

"The cold water slows the decay process," explained Lindsey from his place at the end of the room, anticipating her thoughts.

Louise saw that the running water also carried away, bit by bit, the decay that it could not prevent. In more than one case, a slight stream within the spray had bored a small hole in a forehead, detached a nose, or eroded lips. She studied each body carefully, passing slowly from one to the next. The single cadaver that should have been of greatest interest to her was at the far end, easily distinguishable by the photographic equipment now surrounding it. She felt nonetheless compelled to speculate about the grim circumstances that brought each person to rest in the cold and comfortless indignity of the dead room.

A large, yellowish card at the foot of the slab identified each individual and, where such information was known, the cause of death. Viewing the remains of the unfortunate man who had drowned was the most difficult to bear: a bloated form with an enormous stomach and puffy limbs, it was swollen and blued not only by the water in which it took its last breath, but also by the water now trickling over it. The flesh of the face sloughed off in strips, and bones protruded through rotten skin. What remained was like nothing so much as a lump of discolored, boiled beef. *So much for dust to dust*, she thought. *Better ashes to ashes than this.*

She swallowed back her distress, which was rooted more in empathy for the deceased than in disgust for the gross details of death. She made her way to the body of a young woman of twenty or so, broad and strong, who seemed merely asleep. Her full, white form displayed the most delicate softness of tint. On her seemingly fresh lips appeared a half smile. The whites of her eyes were laced with broken blood vessels. Her head was inclined to one side. Around her neck was a black band, a necklace of shadow. The spidery handwriting on the card at her feet read, *Elizabeth Sheridan / Suicide by hanging.* Perhaps, thought Louise mordantly, she hanged herself after shooting her husband in the forehead.

Next was a great, burly fellow. *Stewart Hopkins / Mason / Fell from scaffolding.* He had a bushy chest, a shaven jaw, a well-nourished body, and a crushed skull. Death had made a deformed statue of him.

"The wound looks different now," Lindsey said, interrupting Louise's communion with the dead. "The surgeon seems to have attempted to restore the skin to its original position. We're fortunate he hasn't started the water."

Louise made her way directly to the last slab in the row, to examine the target of Lindsey's pointing finger.

"If you look closely," he continued, "you'll now see tear lines radiating outward from the bullet entry point. The skin ripped away like the crust of a tart cut from its center."

"So when the bullet entered," she said, "something caused these flaps to peel back and away."

"And the surgeon put them back in place, as best he could," added Lindsey, "to examine the bullet hole, nice and round. That's how I've always seen them before, nice and round, not torn open like this one. Now that the skin is back in place, we should measure the diameter of the hole, which should approximate the diameter of the bullet."

Louise found a pair of calipers on a nearby cart. Lindsey placed them over the reconstructed entry wound, opened the pointers to either side of the bullet hole, and read the measurement.

"Three eighths of an inch." He handed the calipers back to Louise. "Miss Hawkins, see if you can locate the surgeon's autopsy notes while we begin taking photographs. Jeffers, as we are catless, we'll do it my way. We'll begin with the shortest exposure. In this light, I'm guessing at least ten seconds. Then we'll add ten seconds for each subsequent round. I'll position the palm so it faces the cameras. Hopefully the rigor has passed."

Louise could not pull herself away from the fascinating business surrounding the body.

As Jeffers prepared his camera to photograph the hand, Lindsey reached for the dead man's cold left hand, only to realize that Louise had already grasped it with her two warm ones, rotating it so that the palm faced up. "Rigor's passed," she said quietly.

Her fingertips lingered there. She was awed by the chill and the firmness of the flesh. *He's no longer in there*, she thought, wondering where in fact the lieutenant might now be.

"Miss Hawkins," said Lindsey, "I remind you of the autopsy report."

"May I first look through your camera, Mr. Jeffers?" she asked.

"We need you to find the autopsy report," Lindsey interrupted, just as Jeffers was saying, "Certainly."

Louise chose to hear only Jeffers.

"Thank you, sir. I see that you use an American Optical camera box, suitable for six by eight inch plates, with a Dallmeyer lens."

"Six point five by eight point five plates, more precisely," clarified Jeffers, "and a Dallmeyer rapid rectilinear lens, since it is well suited to dimly lit interiors."

Louise lifted the dark cloth and slipped beneath. She looked through the focusing glass at the rear of the camera. Everything was black. Jeffers removed the lens cover, and immediately Louise could see, projected on the slightly frosted focusing glass, a faint, inverted image of Lieutenant Perenna's left hand, covered with the mysterious smudge.

"Is it focused?" asked Jeffers.

"Not quite."

"Then what you must do," explained Jeffers, taking her right hand and moving it to a nearby thumbwheel, "is turn this in whichever direction causes the image to come into focus."

Without removing her head from the beneath the dark cloth, Louise slowly turned the thumbwheel, top edge forward, but the image became more blurry. She then turned the thumbwheel in the opposite direction until the image came into sharp focus, announcing her success with a simple, "There."

Jeffers placed the cap back on the lens, and everything beneath the hood again went dark.

Lindsey continued setting up his camera to photograph the bullet wound, mild aggravation creeping across his face. "Ready," he announced, making it clear that he was waiting on the two of them.

"You can move the dark cloth aside for the moment," continued Jeffers, to Lindsey's dismay. "Now swing the focusing plate out of the way. It latches on the right and hinges on the left."

Louise followed Jeffers's instructions without difficulty. He handed her the first plate.

"Dry plate," he said. "We prepare them ourselves, back at the office, well in advance of any need for them. We can store them indefinitely. Wet plates, on the other hand, are incompatible with the demands of our work."

"Given that you would need to use them," continued Louise, "within five minutes of preparing them, and you would need to develop them immediately, here, in a portable darkroom."

Jeffers smiled at her, acknowledging her perspicacity with a nod. She took the dry plate from him, confidently, and tried to insert it where the focusing glass had just been. To her surprise and mild frustration, though, she was unable to do so.

"May I?" Jeffers asked.

Louise returned the plate without a word. Jeffers flipped it top to bottom then handed it back it to her. She accepted it with a sly grin and quickly slid it into place.

"There," continued Jeffers, pointing to the right edge of the plate, "is where you will grasp the dark slide and remove it, but you will do so only after covering everything with the dark cloth. Step this way just a bit, please. You needn't be under the cloth at this point; just your hand as it pulls the dark slide from the plate."

Louise did as instructed, returning the dark cloth and pulling the dark slide from the plate.

"Now the emulsion will be exposed to any light entering the camera," said Jeffers, "and we will allow light to enter only through the lens."

"I'm ready here," repeated an impatient Lindsey.

"When I say open," continued Jeffers calmly, "after counting down from three, you and Mr. Lindsey will gently but quickly remove the lens cap from your camera. "When I say close, after counting down from nine, you will gently but quickly replace the lens cap."

Louise positioned herself near the front of her camera, assumed the same pose as Lindsey, then nodded to Jeffers that she was ready.

"Three. Two. One. Open."

She removed the lens cap, mimicking Lindsey by holding it well away from the lens.

"One thousand nine."

"One thousand eight."

"One thousand seven."

"One thousand six."

"One thousand five."

"One thousand four."

"One thousand three."

"One thousand two."

"One thousand one."

"Close."

Louise returned the lens cap without difficulty, and Jeffers handed her the dark slide.

"Now," he said, "by carefully reaching under the hood, without admitting any light that will further expose the emulsion, you need to re-insert the dark slide."

Before Jeffers had finished his sentence, Lindsey had already returned his dark slide to his camera. Louise, recognizing the value of experience and practice in the process, handed her dark slide back to Jeffers.

"I have an autopsy report to locate," she said to him, with a slight smile. "Thank you for your time and consideration in assisting me with my first photograph."

Jeffers smiled in return, nodded, took the dark slide, then expertly slid it back into the dry plate, barely disturbing the dark cloth in the process. Louise recovered her crutches, which had been leaning nearby against William Perenna's slab. She hobbled her way to the roll top desk at the far end of the room.

"Next time," said Lindsey to Jeffers, firmly but in a hushed voice, "when I tell you to do something, you will do it."

"I always do, sir," replied a suddenly assertive Jeffers, "including this time. You never instructed me to take the photograph myself. Nor did you forbid me from allowing her to take it. You certainly didn't instruct me to locate the autopsy report. If you choose to be angry at someone for disobeying you, you should be angry with her."

Even as Lindsey's aggravation grew, he tried to understand the cause of it. He questioned whether he should ever have invited Louise to join them in the dead room, since matters suddenly seemed muddled.

"You're smitten with her," he said, suddenly, accusingly.

"And you, sir," replied Jeffers, "have never before questioned the quality of my work, or how I go about it. Why is it that you suddenly question me?"

They stood there momentarily, examining one another, the silence and stench of the room hanging heavily over them.

"Next exposure will be for twenty seconds," said Lindsey, turning back to his camera.

Upon reaching the desk, Louise perused the stacks of paperwork covering it. She could make no immediate sense of their order, so she lowered herself into the stiff wooden chair and scanned the desktop for any paper with "Perenna" written on it.

"Three, two, one, open," she heard Lindsey say from across the room.

She began lifting corners of folios to see if any contained the report of interest, but found nothing. She pulled documents from each of the pigeonholes in turn. Nothing. The drawer, though, held a stack of folios, each unlabeled and lashed with twine. She opened two. Neither held Perenna's autopsy report. When the third folio's flap opened in her hands, she at last saw the marking she had been looking for: *William Perenna / Inquest / 17 March 1879*. Across the room, she could hear the countdown.

"One thousand two."

"One thousand one."

"Close."

"I've found it!" she exclaimed.

"Good," hollered Lindsey, re-inserting his dark slide and swapping the exposed plate for one unexposed. "Thirty seconds this time, Jeffers. Let me know when you're ready."

Jeffers had already finished preparing for his next shot, having intentionally rushed to beat his employer. "Ready and waiting, sir," he said, in mildly acerbic fashion.

At the desk, Louise rose clumsily, arranging the folio and crutches under her arms, and began hobbling towards Lindsey.

"Please, wait there," Lindsey said. "I'll come to you."

Louise froze, unsure of how best to deal with her double-arm encumbrances.

"Open and close both cameras, Jeffers," instructed Lindsey, "one second apart. Now, Miss Hawkins, let's have a look at that report."

Lindsey strode to the desk and slipped the folio from beneath Louise's arm. Propping the documents in one hand like a book, he paged through them rapidly, muttering between periodic glances at his watch.

He snapped the folio shut. "You have seven minutes to copy this report. Can you write that quickly?"

"I think so," she said, though she had no idea how long the report was.

"Then please do so," he said, dropping the report on the desk and turning back to the photography.

Louise returned to the chair and plopped into it. Sliding a sheet from a thick pile of blank paper, she took a pen from its holder, opened the inkwell, dipped the pen, then hesitated.

"Do you want me to copy every particular?" she asked, suddenly daunted by all the scratchings that comprised the report.

"It is your task to accomplish. You decide how to best perform it within your constraints. You now have six and a half minutes to make that copy. Jeffers, please check on Mr. Hawkins in the alley? We'll want his help when we pack up the equipment and get the hell out of here."

Jeffers moved briskly from the room, Lindsey returned to the cameras, and Louise began writing.

> *The body is that of a well-developed, well-nourished male identified to me as William Perenna of 22 Torquay Terrace. The height is 72 inches and the weight is 13.5 stones. Light brown, closely cropped hair covers the scalp. The irises are blue. The teeth are unremarkable.*

Lindsey returned to his camera just before Jeffers returned to his.

"He will not be of much help, sir," said Jeffers.

"Alright. You rotate the hand so that we can capture the back of it. I'll reset my camera to photograph the genitals."

Startled by the word, Louise looked up in spite of herself, and then remembered her task.

> *Rigor mortis is well developed and generalized. Livor mortis is faint and posterior, mostly in the buttocks and legs. Livor mortis is mostly fixed but*

blanches when pressed with the thumb. The corneas are clear.

In the background, Louise could hear the sounds of plates being shuffled and countdowns being synchronized.

Gunshot entry and exit wounds lie in the head, and these will be described in greater detail subsequently. Stains of copious bloody fluid exude from the ear canals, the nostrils, and the mouth.

"We will start the sequence of exposures over again, beginning with ten seconds. Ready?

"Ready."

"Three, two, one open."

The fingernails are intact. The upper extremities are notable for the left hand, which is heavily sooted. Also, a reddened area, possibly a burn, exists along the web between the thumb and index finger of the left hand.

She scribbled furiously as countdowns were synchronized and plates were swapped.

The neck and trunk reveal no recent injuries.

The external genitalia are remarkable for a single, firm ulceration on the penis. The ulceration is oval shaped, 1¼ in. long and ¼ in. wide. The ulceration has the clean base and sharp borders of a chancre.

"He was in the first stage of syphilis," said Lindsey flatly, approaching the desk to peer over Louise's shoulder. In the background, Jeffers continued taking the necessary photographs, moving smoothly, almost effortlessly, between the two cameras.

Louise dipped her pen, determined not to be rattled by all that was going on about her.

A gunshot wound is present in the forehead. The entry wound lies 3 in, beneath the top of the head, along the front midline. Gaping radially oriented lacerations extend into the skin.

She thought of how ghastly these tears looked even when restored, and how much worse they had looked at the scene, when the lieutenant's lifeblood was still flowing from his unbreathing form.

Upon restoring these lacerated triangles to their original position, a gunshot entry wound measuring about 7/16 in. in diameter is seen. Multiple dark particles, which under a microscope appear to be gunpowder particles, adhere to the skin of the face, mostly around the nose, cheeks, and temples.

"Finished here, sir," announced Jeffers, as he completed his final countdown. Louise could hear plates being stacked, lenses being removed and packed, camera boxes being collapsed, tripod legs being compressed.

The wound track travels directly from front to back.

The facial structures reveal palpable fractures. A 5½ in. long horizontal laceration lies in the rear scalp, and two additional shorter lacerations extend from the midportion of this defect.

These lacerations fit together upon replacement. The confluence of these lacerations lies along the rear midline 2¾ in. beneath the top of the head.

"Miss Hawkins, have you been listening?" asked Lindsey. "You are aware of the time, I presume. I would prefer not to be caught in here."

Cause of death is a gunshot wound to the forehead. Death was instantaneous. The diameter of the entry wound is consistent with a bullet fired from the Colt .36 caliber revolver found at the scene.

"Jeffers, let's get this equipment and our friend in the alley to the cart. Miss Hawkins, are you finished?"

Her handwriting crabbed with haste as she hurried to get down the report's concluding lines.

"One moment, Mr. Lindsey!"

Autopsy performed by Dr Daniel Weston at the mortuary of the Bristol Police Central Station on this 15th day of March 1879. Report prepared by same.

She returned the pen to its holder, closed the inkwell, then entwined the original report folio and placed it back in the drawer.

"We must leave," said Lindsey as he doused the lights.

Louise gathered the pages she'd copied and shoved them under her waistband, then stood and hobbled once more past the slabs, trying to ignore the running water and decaying flesh. The stench no longer unsettled her. Odd. She stole a passing peek at the young woman who had hanged herself. Lindsey extinguished the last light, and they quit the dead room, passing into the dark of the alley, where the rank city air tasted sweet in comparison.

———✦———

Early morning, Sunday 16 March 1879
Bristol Police Central Station, Bridewell Street
Bristol, England

John Reeves stepped from the shadows of the internal passageway that led to the dead room. He had been working late in his office, having no particular reason to go home. He had been drawn to the dead room by some subliminal unease, an unease that he now realized had been stirred by the opening of the alley door, and by the consequent movement of death-tainted air. He had quietly observed the activity of the three unauthorized investigators, paying particular interest in Louise Hawkins, admiring her calm competence.

He stood gazing into the dead room, having, at that time, no place where he was wanted or needed.

chapter four

MR. JEREMY HAWKINS

SUNDAY MORNING, 16 MARCH 1879
FIRST-CLASS CARRIAGE,
    ENROUTE TO GLOUCESTER CENTRAL STATION
EIGHT MILES NORTH OF BRISTOL, ENGLAND

The steam whistle wailed as the engine thundered past Westleigh. The pastoral scenery outside the windows was distorted by streaks of rainwater running diagonally across the outside of the glass.

"Thank you for joining me," said Louise to Lindsey, "and for the first-class tickets. I appreciate your willingness to share all of this with my brother Jeremy. Since you like being around people who are a bit different, I suspect you will like him a great deal. He is the most different person I know."

"If he can provide some insight into these photographs and autopsy report, as you claim," said Lindsey, "then this trip will certainly be worth the time and money."

"Did you sleep at all?" Louise asked.

"I needed to get these photographs developed. I had only enough time to pop in at home, to bathe, explain to Isabella why I'm missing church yet again, give Adeline a kiss, and rush to the station."

"Your wife and daughter?" inquired Louise.

"Yes," said Lindsey, in such a way to engender a few minutes' silence.

"I think I must dispose of my clothes from last night," said Louise. "That awful stench, it clings to them, even after a vigorous scrubbing with disinfecting soap. Mrs. Croton, my landlady, wanted to burn them on the spot. But I can't very well dispose of my hair, can I? I spent some hours this morning washing it repeatedly. It's just recently dry."

Lindsey watched the rivulets of water veining the window glass.

"I don't intend to be boring," Louise continued after a pause. "Did the photographs turn out as you wished?"

"Explain to me again," he responded, "why a man in an asylum should be able to make sense of that which no one else can."

"Actually, Barnwood House is a private hospital," Louise said, deflecting his question by answering one not asked.

"A rose by any other name," Lindsey said.

Louise pretended not to chafe at his observation. He feigned sleep, which became the real thing within minutes, and they rode together in silence.

———※———

EIGHTEEN YEARS EARLIER
THURSDAY EVENING, 18 APRIL 1861
SOUTHFIELD COTTAGE, LECKHAMPTON ROAD
LECKHAMPTON, ENGLAND

"May I sit with you while you study, Jeremy?" asked four-year-old Louise, pulling a three-legged stool beside the wing chair in which her brother perched.

"If you're quiet."

She sat quietly for a small eternity, her restlessness increasing as she sat.

"What are you reading?"

"Pascal's *Pensées*. Now shh!"

She sat quietly for another endless span.

"I'm four. I'll be five in three hundred and fifty-seven days."

Jeremy nodded and continued reading.

"When were you born?" she asked.

"Eighteen hundred and forty-eight."

"So you're probably twelve, maybe thirteen. What day were you born on?"

"Twenty-nine February." Exasperation was detectable in his voice.

"Thirteen then," said Louise. She went silent only briefly as the fingers on her right hand danced against her thumb.

"You're three thousand three hundred and twenty-six days older than me," she exclaimed.

"No, I'm three thousand three hundred and twenty-*eight* days older than you. You forgot that '52 and '56 were leap years."

Her shoulders slumped and a frown replaced her smile as she said, "I'll never be as smart as you."

"I suspect you'll be proven wrong about that as well."

The smile returned, and she sat quietly long enough for Jeremy to finish two full pages of Pascal. Outside, a bird sang in the spring rain. From far off came the sound of the neighboring boys' laughter.

"Why don't you play with the other boys?" she asked.

"They don't like me because I'm smarter than they are."

"Will people not like me?" she asked, suddenly concerned.

Jeremy put a bookmark between the pages and closed the covers slowly as he composed his response. He looked directly into her tiny face. She looked directly back, worried, her future hanging in the balance.

"It would probably be best if you didn't try to convince everyone of how smart you are. People don't like others who are too different. You don't have to pretend you're a cretin or anything, just don't let them know about you being a genius."

She looked so sad it broke his heart.

"You can be brilliant around me, though," he said. "I will love you all the more for it."

She wrapped her tiny arms around his neck.

SUNDAY MORNING, 16 MARCH 1879
GLOUCESTER CENTRAL STATION
GLOUCESTER, ENGLAND

At the cabstand outside the station, Lindsey held an umbrella over both Louise and himself while signaling a four-wheeler. He helped Louise up before informing the driver of their destination. He then closed his umbrella, lifted his portmanteau, and climbed in beside Louise.

"I apologize for my insensitivity before," he said. "I'm tired, there's trouble at the paper, and Isabella is irritated with me, but that gives me no excuse."

"Jeremy is not in Barnwood because he is *non compos mentis*," said Louise, only slightly appeased. "On the contrary, he is the sanest person I know. In fact, it was in part his cleverness that brought him there. He is so much an intellectual superior to all around him that they shun him or poke fun at him. As a boy, he never developed friendships and never learned how to behave with anyone other than our parents and siblings, so he withdrew into his own world."

"I understand," said Lindsey, in a softened tone. "I actually do understand about being different, and I apologize for being so brusque. Perhaps it was my lack of sleep."

"Or perhaps you were merely speaking your mind?" said Louise without bitterness.

"Perhaps that."

"It was when the epilepsy overcame him that my parents were left with little choice in the matter. Barnwood is widely recognized as one of the best institutions of its kind and, for a burdensome fee, cares for Jeremy in comfortable surroundings. He is as content there as might be possible for him anywhere, free to amass and organize all manner of information, pursue answers to the greatest of mathematical puzzles, attempt to extend Euclid's method to all of human reason, calculate pi to hundreds of places, and explore other challenges that some might regard as queer."

"And you truly believe he will be able to provide insight into our mystery?"

"More likely than not."

"Will he not shy away from me, as he does from everyone else?"

"Keep the discussion focused on our indecipherable mystery and he will be glad to speak with you all day. Wander off into personal matters, and he will turn silent on you. Only mother and I can be tender with him without causing him distress."

"Is he likely to have a seizure in the midst of our discussion, if you don't mind my being so blunt?"

"It's possible, of course, but not likely. He's explained to me that the time between seizures is seemingly random and still unpredictable. He believes, though, that he might eventually be able to approximate the intervals between seizures with an exponential equation. Until he solves that thorny problem, we assume that the seizures occur randomly, with an average, for him, of one every week or so. That is, if he is not taking his bromide."

"Bromide?"

"Potassium bromide. It's the only substance known to significantly reduce the frequency of epileptic seizures. It's a palliative, not a cure, but it can cut the rate by fifty percent, even more in some cases."

"But he apparently does not take it as he should," observed Lindsey.

"It dulls him. He would rather have his wits about him and seize once a week than lessen his mental capacity so that he might have only a few seizures each month."

"A Faustian bargain," said Lindsey, "with Mephistopheles visiting once a week."

"Hardly that. Epilepsy is a disease, not the work of the Devil. Common misunderstanding of it finally brought Jeremy to isolate himself. It is difficult enough being so bright, as I suspect you know, but it is a far greater burden being brilliant and epileptic." Their eyes held each other's at this tacit compliment, and then, with a mutual impulse, they turned to the scenery outside to break the intimacy.

The rain had stopped. The countryside was bountiful and the livestock content to graze in the damp grass. Louise and Lindsey traveled the next mile in silence, save for the soft clop of horseshoes and the occasional creak of a coach spring.

"What did you think of the little adventure last night?" Lindsey asked suddenly.

Louise pondered before answering.

"It was more than I can sort out still, horrible and strangely fascinating at the same time. I know I am supposed to be revolted by the details and the immodesty, but I was not. I was simultaneously engrossed, mentally stimulated, and intrigued. There is both guilt and pride in my breast, for my participation. I promised myself to never again do such a thing, and now I fear I will never again have the opportunity. I try to put my mind on other matters, but when I am not otherwise engaged, it is all I can think of."

"That will fade. Somewhat. In part. Eventually," Lindsey said, with a dour expression.

SUNDAY MORNING, 16 MARCH 1879
BARNWOOD HOUSE HOSPITAL, BARNWOOD ROAD
BARNWOOD, ENGLAND

The rural Barnwood House Hospital was only a mile and a half east of Central Station, so the ride there required slightly less than twenty minutes. Situated just south of Barnwood Road, the hospital consisted of the only substantial collection of buildings in the area. As the cab approached from the west, Lindsey studied the three-story main building while Louise provided details of its history and operation.

"Barnwood House was constructed, early this century, as a gentleman's residence," she began, "by one Robert Morris who lived in nearby Barnwood Court. A few decades ago, the house was transformed into a hospital by extending the wings on either side of the central block. The hospital first opened its doors to patients almost twenty years ago—nineteen years and two months, to be more precise."

The cab turned onto the broad path that led towards the entry, passing by lush gardens on either side.

"There are approximately one hundred resident patients," continued Louise, "divided nearly evenly between men and women. The men occupy the eastern wing, there. Women have that one there, to our right. There are four categories of patients, each housed according to his categorization. Category Four patients require constant supervision. Category One patients, such as Jeremy, are free to wander the grounds as they like, and to partake of all facilities open to the patients. There are a recreation room, a library, an arboretum, a chapel, and even two tennis courts. The food is plentiful and well prepared. The heating, ventilation, and sanitation are all excellent. Under Dr. Needham's supervision, the cure rate has been remarkable. At county asylums, the cure rate last year averaged thirty-nine percent. For private institutions, the average was forty-nine percent. At Barnwood, the cure rate was fifty-three percent. Of course, as a private hospital, they are privileged to choose which patients they admit, and to define *cure* in whatever form they choose, so those statistics may not be as praiseworthy as the administrators would have them appear, scientifically speaking."

The cab veered left, to follow the circular final approach to the building. It stopped directly in front of the entryway, but no one came out to greet them. Lindsey climbed from the cab with his closed umbrella and his densely packed portmanteau. He set down the bag, propped the umbrella against it, and helped Louise descend. Once she was steady on her crutches, he paid the cabman and sent him on his way. Lifting his belongings, he led Louise up the stairs and through the main doors.

"Good morning, Mr. Talmage," Louise greeted the attendant standing behind the large reception counter. Talmage was writing something in a logbook.

"Good to see you again, Miss Hawkins," he replied, looking up, surprised. "Crutches! Nothing too serious, I hope."

"Just a minor sprain," said Louise.

"Good, good," he said, trying to ignore the injuries to her forehead. "All has been well with Jeremy. He's been quieter than usual, engrossed now, it seems, with some more complex mathematics. He's in his room. Good that we situated him on the ground floor, lest I be carting you up and down the stairs."

"This is Mr. Lindsey," said Louise, "a friend who's been helping me in my time of need."

Lindsey nodded absentmindedly, as he gazed around at the stately grand entrance, apparently largely unchanged from its days as a gentleman's retreat.

"That's kind of you, sir," said Talmage. "We encourage guests here at Barnwood House. Please let me know if I can assist you in any way."

"I'm not sure how long we might be," said Louise, "but we absolutely must return to Bristol sometime today."

"Feel free to lunch with us, if you wish. Check in at the coach house whenever you're ready to leave, and we'll see to it that you get back to the station."

"You're very kind, Mr. Talmage, as usual. Thank you again."

He nodded acknowledgement, then went back to his writing. Louise turned and made her way down the broad, well-lit hallway. Lindsey followed.

Jeremy's room was on the left, slightly more than halfway to the end. Louise knocked. "Jeremy, it's Louise."

From within came the sounds of chair legs scraping along floorboards and a faint shuffling of soft shoes across a carpeted floor. The door swung open enthusiastically.

"I'm so glad you're—" Jeremy's lips seemed to spasm, and his voice fell when he spied Lindsey standing behind his sister. His slackened countenance, surprisingly hale for a long-term hospital patient, revealed crow's feet, wrinkles, and hollows that belied his thirty-one years.

Though not startlingly handsome, Jeremy Hawkins had an undeniable physical presence that challenged conventional description. His pale skin and remarkable amber eyes set his other features into the background. His curly brown hair, aquiline nose, and slightly squared jaw came to attention only after one pulled focus from his eyes.

He was attired neither as patient nor a gentleman, rather as someone too busy to bother with formality or social decorum:

a machine-made cotton shirt in white, with long sleeves and a simple turned-down collar; no ascot or other decoration about the neck; and his plain black trousers leading downward to brightly colored Persian slippers.

"This is David Lindsey," Louise said. "He's a newspaper publisher and reporter."

Jeremy noted her lumpy, bruised forehead, her crutches, and her bulbous ankle bandage. His eyes flicked to Lindsey.

"It's merely sprained," Louise said, "not broken. I managed to do it all to myself the day before yesterday. More importantly, we have a problem that I suspect only you can solve."

"Mathematical?" he asked, clearly intrigued by her statement. Life came back into his face as he focused on Louise, the bearer of a challenge.

"Criminal."

"The only thing better," he said, stepping back and pulling the door open, examining Lindsey from hair to shoes. He pointed to an iron stand. "You may place your umbrella there. Set your case beside it."

The room was of a good size, almost as large as Louise's apartment, crowded in the extreme, but deftly organized. Every inch of wall space was occupied by crude, sturdy bookshelves stretching from floor to ceiling. Nearly every inch of shelving was filled with books, in some places they were stacked two-deep or shoved on top of the standing books.

No close inspection was needed to perceive that the shelves' contents were arranged by subject matter. Labels had been affixed to the fronts of the shelves with the volumes further ordered by the authors' last names. The shelving was interrupted only by the entry door and a single window on the opposite wall, facing the front of the building. The shelves continued both over and under the window. Even the bed, near the umbrella stand, was set away from the walls to accommodate shelving.

Magazines, stacked a dozen high, filled the space under the bed. They also lined the floor along the foot of the bookshelves, leaving a gap only in front of the window where a well-used reading chair sat empty, facing the door to allow the daylight illumination of reading matter, as well as providing a misanthrope's view of the entryway.

Near the center of the room was a table of medium size, three sides of which were set with simple wooden chairs. Occupying the fourth side, the one nearest the door and lacking a chair, were lines of journals held upright by stout stone bookends, each having one face cut flat, polished to highlight the colorful minerals inside. On the far side of the table, nearest the reading chair, rested a large journal opened just past midpoint, its left-hand page teeming with figures of mathematical calculations, its upper right-hand page nearly as crowded.

"I see you're still chasing Shanks's record," said Louise, examining the open journal.

"It's my default task, and it's turned quite exciting. I think he may have made an error at position four hundred and sixty-nine. He calculated it as an eight. I think it should be a nine and I'm in the process of double-checking my own work. It will take another day or two, but if I'm correct, I will have calculated pi with more precision than anyone before."

Louise tossed her crutches aside and hopped to wrap her arms around his waist, squeezing affectionately. He stood awkwardly, trying to wrap his arms around her.

"I'm so proud of you," she said before releasing him, unperturbed by his weak response to her hug. She drew back and looked at him. "You thought you would have to go out beyond six hundred and seven."

Lindsey stared at them in confused amazement, so Louise tried to explain.

"He's using Machin's formula to calculate pi. Machin described his approach in seventeen hundred and six, I think it was, and he used it to become the first person to calculate pi to one hundred places. More recently William Shanks used Machin's formula to calculate pi out to six hundred and seven places. He published his work in fifty-three. Jeremy has long been attempting to calculate pi out to seven hundred decimal places, not knowing if he will be able to do so in his lifetime. So this little surprise, therefore, is quite exciting."

"I'm sorry," Lindsey said, shaking his head, bewildered but impressed. "Your maths skills are clearly beyond mine."

Louise turned back to Jeremy.

"You're looking wonderful," she said, beaming. She reached up and unsuccessfully attempted to flatten his unruly hair. "Except for this mess."

He ducked aside with a shy smile and offered her the chair next to his at the table

"Tell me about your mystery," he said, eager to move past introductions and pleasantries.

All three seated themselves. Jeremy closed his journal and placed it atop the others, thus creating a clear space about which the three of them could crowd.

"John and I were walking along Torquay Terrace Friday morning, as were, coincidentally, Mr. Lindsey and his employee, Mr. Jeffers. We all heard a gunshot fired within a house nearby, and entered it to find an expectant mother standing in the front room, a pistol on the floor before her, and her dead husband on the floor beyond the pistol. Mr. Jeffers managed to take an underexposed photograph of the body before the police, ah, how should I say, *encouraged* him to leave. Much better photographs of the body were obtained early this morning, in the police station's dead room. We have these, as well as a copy of the autopsy report. While it seems clear that the woman shot the man, certain aspects of the shooting mystify us, and we hope you might provide some insight."

Lindsey placed his portmanteau on his lap and began extracting books and magazines.

"I almost forgot," said Louise. "I've brought you some additional reading material. Or perhaps I should say that Mr. Lindsey has brought them to you, since he toted them all this way for me. Thank you for that, Mr. Lindsey."

Jeremy looked over the books and magazines quickly, almost smiling when he saw Louise's worn copy of *Agricola* and the hefty *Scientific American* supplement.

"Wonderful," he said sincerely, tossing the reading material on the bed. "All right, show me the information in the sequence it developed. First, the photograph from the house."

Lindsey laid the photograph on the table. From her purse, Louise brought forth a magnifying glass and handed it to Jeremy, who leaned over and examined the photograph through the lens.

"It's not well exposed," he observed.

"We were working under less than ideal circumstances," explained Lindsey.

"Of course. But it's not only underexposed, it is slightly out of focus—assuming, of course, that your point of primary interest was the head wound."

"Yes, that bullet hole is one of our puzzlements."

"Because it's torn open," observed Jeremy, "not round, as it should be."

"Precisely," agreed Lindsey, impressed by Jeremy's quick insight.

"So you have some knowledge of guns and the wounds they cause," noted Jeremy, without looking up.

"I'm a reporter. I deal in the behavior of humans."

"I can imagine where that might lead," said Jeremy. "These stains on the hand, do you wonder about them as well?"

"That's the other mystery," said Louise.

Jeremy studied the photograph a bit longer before receiving the autopsy report. With a glance at the handwriting, he aimed a quizzical look at his sister, who responded only by shrugging one shoulder and smiling ephemerally. He grunted.

"The surgeon describes the material on the hand as soot," said Jeremy, reading, "but makes no effort to detail it further."

Louise held up a hand when Lindsey moved to comment. They sat in silence until Jeremy reached the surgeon's conclusions.

"So it was a bullet entry wound, but the blast was so powerful that it peeled the skin away in folds." Jeremy thought for a moment, and then said, "Now show me your proper photographs of that wound."

Lindsey pulled out his three photographs of the entry wound.

"Three different exposure times," said Jeremy. "That's thoughtful work. You took these? The longest exposure came out the best, yet still it is a bit underexposed. How long was that exposure?"

"Thirty seconds."

"I would have guessed it would need a bit longer. Your care paid off." Looking again through the magnifying glass, he continued, "I can see that the surgeon reapproximated the wound by putting the torn flesh back in its original position to reveal this seven-sixteenth-inch diameter hole. Let's see the photographs of the hand."

Lindsey handed him the six photographs. Jeremy riffled through them, immediately perceived the proper way to organize them, then laid them out in an arrangement of three by two. Using the glass, he began slowly scanning over every square inch of them.

"Once again, I compliment the thoughtfulness of your work. Photographs of both sides of the hand, three exposures each side. Nearly sufficient."

After several minutes of study, without looking up, he extended his hand for other evidence in Lindsey's bag.

Lindsey reached hesitantly into his portmanteau and passed the last three photographs to Jeremy, who gave them but a moment's attention before dropping them on the table, as if uninterested.

"He was newly syphilitic," Jeremy remarked. He turned to Louise, considered something, then, without looking from his sister, said to Lindsey, "You think that is relevant, else you would not have taken the pictures."

"The woman is pregnant, by seven or eight months," said Lindsey. "Her husband was an army lieutenant, just returned from fourteen months abroad. Other newspapers have reported her pregnancy, which is obvious to all, using her infidelity to asperse her character beyond what the evidence at hand permits—as bad as that evidence already seems. My colleagues, however, don't yet know about the syphilis. The prosecution does, or soon will. I'm not sure what they might choose to do with it—perhaps use it as her motive for shooting him, perhaps suppress it for fear of making her sympathetic to the jurors."

"I find it a tedious nothing," said Jeremy, finally turning to Lindsey. "Focus on the evidence resulting from the shooting. Get back into that house. Measure the height of the bullet hole from the floor, and measure the distance between the wall and where Louise first apprehended the pregnant woman. Draw a sketch to show where the victim lay and where the revolver was in comparison to both parties. Include distances. Consider the trigonometry. Louise will help you with that. You'll find some of your answers there."

Lindsey began to respond, but Jeremy cut him short.

"Get yourself a Colt 1851 Navy revolving pistol, thirty-six caliber. They made some twenty thousand here in England, at the London Armory. Do not assume any other gun will suffice. You must get the exact type of weapon that was used in the Torquay Terrace shooting. You'll also need a few score cartridges, slightly oversized, three-seven-five caliber, and some percussion caps, number ten size. Take the revolver and accessories, your camera, and a half dozen fresh pigs' heads to some remote location. Fire the bullets into the pigs' heads from various distances—first from ten feet, then five, then one, then with the muzzle pressed firmly against the skin, and finally with the gun fired directly alongside the head. Take photographs of the wounds. Study them. You'll find more answers there."

"That doesn't sound like it will require forty bullets," said Lindsey, gathering up his photographs.

"For anyone experienced firing the weapon," replied Jeremy flatly, "a half dozen would do. Are you perchance an adept marksman, Mr. Lindsey?"

"Ah, well, what might you consider adept?"

"I thought as much. I therefore recommend that you purchase three score cartridges, and try not to shoot yourself. You are in for a considerable surprise. Share your results with me if you wish, but I already know what happened. Thank you for your visit, but I do have other matters demanding my attention. It has been a pleasure meeting you, Mr. Lindsey. Louise, may we speak in private?"

Lindsey was flummoxed by this abrupt dismissal. "How, how, how—" he stammered, never completing his sentence.

"These data," said Jeremy. "They tell the story to anyone who can read them. If you follow my recommendations, you will understand them much more clearly than if I simply told you the answer."

Questions raced through Lindsey's head, disabling him by their multitude, the weight of them confining him to his chair.

"Good day, sir," said Jeremy, making clear Lindsey was to leave.

Of the many questions racing through his head, Lindsey surprised even himself with the one he chose to ask: "Why calculate pi to so many places?"

Jeremy stared at him blankly.

"Right," said Lindsey, clearing his throat. "I'll wait outside. Good luck getting to seven hundred."

After Lindsey pulled the door closed behind him, Jeremy spoke bluntly to his sister. "What is going on?"

"I happened to be nearby when the shooting took place," she said. "The woman seemed so heartsick and so alone, I just tried to—"

"That's not what I'm talking about."

"Oh," she said. After brief consideration, she spoke again. "I know it was improper of me to visit the dead room, but John was with me. For some of the time at least. He was ill at—"

"That's not it either," Jeremy sighed.

"All right. I think I understand. I tried not to look at the bodies' sexes too much."

Jeremy frowned. "You mean you don't know?"

"Know what?"

"Lindsey."

"What about Lindsey?"

"He's a woman."

Louise stared at him, rendered speechless. Her brother smiled at her confusion.

"You didn't note the height, the voice, the lack of laryngeal prominence, the total absence of facial hair, the bindings beneath the shirt, the infrequent use of the word *the*?"

Thoughts raced through Louise's head.

"He has a wife and a child," she insisted. "At least he said he did. He's asked me to dine with them this evening."

"Well, if there is a child, it's not of his issue."

"Are you certain?"

Jeremy laughed, a single, deep, delighted yelp. "My dear, beloved Louise. How can you be so brilliant and so oblivious at the same time? Maybe you're the one who belongs here in Barnwood House."

chapter five

MRS. ISABELLA LINDSEY

Sunday evening, 16 March 1879
33 Orchard Street
Bristol, England

Watching her husband's cab pull up in front of their house, Isabella Lindsey positioned herself in the foyer, smoothed her dress, patted her hair one last time, took a deep breath, then prepared herself to smile at the mysterious woman who had captured her husband's time and attention.

Outside, David Lindsey held Louise's crutches as she used the railing to steady herself while hopping up the three front steps. At the top, he returned the crutches, opened the front door, and stopped dead as his wife stood in the doorway, unmoving. When he stepped aside to introduce the two women to one another, Isabella pre-empted him.

"It is so wonderful to meet you, Miss Hawkins," said Mrs. Lindsey to her guest. "Doddy has told me so much about you."

David Lindsey winced at hearing his wife openly speak her pet name for him. Louise stifled a smirk.

"Please, call me Louise."

"And you, please, do call me Isabella. Come through and we'll get you seated comfortably. Doddy, help her up the stoop."

"I've heard more than a bit about you," said Louise, making her own way into the foyer. "You are every bit as lovely as I have been told to expect."

Beautiful and elegant, the hostess was also decorous, acting as if she had never before heard such a compliment.

"That is very generous of you," she said. "After five years of marriage, Doddy still plays the smitten suitor, exaggerating the charms of the one he loves."

"I would not rush to discourage such behavior," said Louise.

"Of course not. He's a dear," said Isabella, dazzling her husband with her smile. Unfurling a graceful arm to indicate the direction, she added, "We will sit in the parlor and get you off that agonized foot. Doddy told me how you injured it. I'll ring for tea."

"I'll just peep in on Adeline," Lindsey said, bounding up the stairs.

"He absolutely adores her," Isabella said, tinkling a small bell as she and Louise relocated to the parlor. "He dotes on her endlessly."

The housekeeper, carrying the tea tray, met them there. She waited for Isabella and Louise to sit beside the tea table before setting the tray onto it.

"The hyson, please," Isabella told her.

From an ornate tea chest, the housekeeper brought forth a ceramic jar, distinctly of Chinese design. She transferred a heap of leaves into the steaming teapot, then returned the jar to its chest.

"Will there be anything else, ma'am?"

"No. Thank you, Mary," said the mistress, and the servant disappeared without a sound.

"This is truly a marvelous room," observed Louise, taking in the parlor's au courant design and furnishings.

"You'll forgive us, I hope," pleaded Isabella with becoming, if patently false, modesty, "for it is still a work in progress, even though we have been here nearly a year. Of course, there is no way we could afford a William Morris protégé to design and furnish our house, so I have relied on my own wits, with no small assistance from Charles Eastlake's *Hints on Household Taste.* I pore over that book so frequently, and so thoroughly, that its pages are very nearly falling out. Once I found Christopher Dresser's *Principles of Decorative Design*, I'm afraid I became incurably afflicted with home decorating."

"You have a gift," said Louise. "The wallpaper, the curtains, the furniture—every bit of it is marvelous."

"You are too kind," said Isabella, with a feigned sense of embarrassment. "I understand that you, on the other hand, are a woman of adventure. To be the first on the scene of a murder! I can hardly imagine. It must have been utterly ghastly. And then to visit that dead house, and in the dead of night, so to speak. How horrid!"

"Your husband had me so busy with scribe's work that I barely had time to notice. I was impressed then, and I remain impressed now, by how efficiently he managed the entire situation. Have you had the opportunity to see him at his work?"

"I have been to the *North Star's* front office on several occasions, but I have only dared peek in back. So much ink and oil and dust and noise! I have found myself too timid to venture further."

"It's quite remarkable, actually. At least it is to me."

"Hopefully it will soon be remarkably profitable. Doddy forewarned me that it could be a year before he brings home more than he spends. I remind him on occasion that our fortune is scarcely boundless."

Lindsey just then descended the stairs, a proud father carrying a small brown-haired girl in his arms.

"This is Adeline," he said.

Isabella poured the tea as Louise rose and hobbled with a single crutch to greet the child.

"Hello, Adeline. I'm Louise."

Adeline gazed back with round brown eyes, her head resting in the crook of her father's neck.

"How old are you?" asked Louise.

Adeline lifted an entire hand of spread digits.

"Five! What a wonderful age," Louise said, moving to take Adeline in her free arm. Lindsey instead set his daughter gently on the floor. Louise smiled as she motioned Adeline to follow her slowly around the room.

"You are just as lovely as your mother," Louise said, noticing that she looked nothing like her father. "What do you think of the furniture she has chosen for this room? What a marvelous tea cabinet. Do you know what it's made of?"

Adeline touched the cabinet gingerly with a quick glance at her mother, as if she'd been previously cautioned not to touch, before shyly answering, "Wood."

"That's right. This type of wood is called bird's-eye maple, but not because it has any birds' eyes in it. That would be silly. Someone just decided that these dark bits look like birds' eyes, but they're not. They are just dark swirls in the wood, beautiful dark swirls."

Adeline reached out and ran her fingers over the surface of the tea cabinet again. "Birds' eyes," she echoed quietly.

"No one can tell from the outside of a maple tree if the wood on the inside will have this surprising pattern. Only when the sawyer cuts into the tree can he tell whether it holds the bird's-eye surprise."

"And the bird's-eye price," said Lindsey.

"Tosh, Doddy," said Isabella, with a smile. "I only purchase what I can get at a bargain."

Louise took in the front of cabinet, as did Adeline, now dragging her fingers along the wood.

"I do adore the simplicity of the design," Louise said, half to the toddler. "Many people prefer furniture that is showy and ponderous, and that sort of design is called *handsome*. Others appreciate curved shapes of *elegant* style, or its frail cousin, *graceful* style, but this tea cabinet is of simple and good design, without ostentatious display of ornament. It pretends to be neither any more nor any less than what it is: *neat*."

"Neat," Adeline murmured, as she continued to feel the wood.

"Others may prefer handsome or elegant, or even graceful," said Louise to her young student, "but I like my tea cabinets to be neat. How about you?"

"Neat," proclaimed Adeline.

"I see you have read Eastlake," said Isabella, delighted.

"A number of years ago," said Louise. "Enough that I can't remember the details particularly well. As an example of my poor recollection, I don't remember Eastlake saying anything about maple."

Louise settled again into her chair. There was enough room in it that Adeline climbed up to settle beside her. Louise took a biscuit from the tea tray and offered it to the little girl, who thanked her and promptly began to nibble all around the edge of the biscuit.

"He seemed to prefer oak, as I recall," Louise went on, "left unvarnished until the grain had enriched and darkened."

"It is de rigueur to design with the dark woods," said Isabella, "but I prefer the lightness of the maple. I find it absurd that we delight in bright days outside, then mimic gloomy days indoors."

"Well, I have learned something from you already," said Louise, sipping tea while Adeline worked at her biscuit. "Now that I have seen the bird's-eye close up, and experienced the uplifting effect of this bright room, I have a new appreciation for what might be done."

"Thank you," Isabella said, charmed by the woman she had expected to dislike.

Lindsey took the chair next to his wife, along with a cup of tea and a biscuit. With the biscuit between his lips, he waved at Adeline with his free fingers and winked. The little girl giggled at her silly father.

Her father, thought Louise.

"You certainly have a way with children," Isabella said. "Adeline is remarkably bashful. She never takes to strangers, yet she seems perfectly at ease with you."

Louise stroked Adeline's hair. "I adore children," she said, "and they sense that. I have none of my own, of course, and none of my half-dozen siblings have yet to produce a niece or nephew for me, so I have no one on whom to lavish attentions."

"I have already heard about your brother Jeremy," said Isabella. "Such a tragedy."

Lindsey cringed. "Darling, I—"

"Hardly that," replied Louise evenly. "A phenomenon, rather. He suffers hardship to be sure, but who among us is free from hardship? He is blessed with gifts greater than most receive."

"Yes, quite so," said Isabella. Then, after a pause, added, "I can only imagine how full your mother's hands were if your other siblings were as precocious as you and Jeremy must have been."

"My mother is a remarkable woman," said Louise. "She was married at nineteen to my father, who was then a landed farmer living directly across the River Severn. Theirs was a pragmatic pairing, my father being the last Hawkins with any hope of carrying on the family line. He was nearly fifty, you see. His only brother had recently passed to his reward without issue. His only sister, my aunt, was not only unmarried, but also well beyond childbearing age. My father rented much of his land to other farmers, but he insisted on working a portion of it himself. He needed an heir. He married my mother and they produced a girl and two boys within three years. The rest of us appeared at roughly two-year intervals. She was with child or nursing, or both, for nearly fifteen years without interruption, giving new life without ever first having had an opportunity to live her own."

"Oh, my," Isabella breathed. She seemed nonplussed at hearing what most considered the pinnacle of womanhood being described as hardship and deprivation.

"Mother saw to it that my sisters and I were not married off in the same fashion, that all of her children benefited from opportunities which had been denied to her. Though my father had come from a long line of farmers, and pursued that avocation by choice rather than out of necessity, by the time John, the youngest, was born, we had settled in Leckhampton, near Cheltenham. Our home was a mere stone's throw from churches, universities, libraries, academies, clubs, societies, gardens, and spas. I was tutored or schooled, or both, throughout my childhood. John and I, in fact, both attended schools not far from here, he at St. Michael's and I at Badminton."

"How impressive," Isabella remarked. "We have heard of Badminton's prestige, of course. Your father did well to provide such a high-quality education for you."

"Father went blind when I was still young," Louise went on.

"Oh, dear," Isabella responded, not certain what else to say. She refilled Louise's teacup without asking.

"Mother not only cared for him, along with the rest of us, she managed the household in Leckhampton and the family lands spread across Gloucestershire and Wales. She handled the land both before and after his death. When Jeremy's epilepsy settled on him, she researched the disease and its treatment. It is she who pays for his current living arrangements at Barnwood House, and they suit him as best as anyone might hope. She visits him frequently, too, and takes him out on holidays from time to time. Now that John has become consumptive—"

Isabella gasped, holding fingers to her lips.

"—she is teaching herself all she can about that affliction, and searching for its best treatment. At this moment, she is in Ventnor, on the Isle of Wight, assessing what is called its therapeutic air, in addition to the conditions and effectiveness of its sanatorium. John was visiting when we became entangled in the tragedy on Torquay Terrace. He will soon depart to rejoin mother in Ventnor. In sum, Isabella, I admire my mother as much as I love her. I hope to make her proud by living my life to its fullest."

The parlor's only sound was a ticking clock.

"Forgive me," said Louise. "I have taken up too much of our visit telling you of my family history."

"Not at all," said Isabella. She rang her bell in three slow movements and a young woman, apparently Adeline's nanny, descended the stairs.

"Come along now, little one," said the woman, brushing crumbs from Adeline's pinafore and lifting the child from the chair. "Say good night to everyone."

Adeline waved at Louise.

"Good night, Adeline," said Louise. "It was a pleasure to meet you."

"Neat," Adeline said with a tiny smile.

Eighteen years earlier
Saturday morning, 6 April 1861
Southfield Cottage, Leckhampton Road
Leckhampton, England

"Can I sit with you while you do your sewing, Mama?" asked three-year-old Louise Hawkins.

"If you don't ask too many questions, dear."

"Why can't Papa see anymore?"

"Because his eyes are quite old now."

"How old are they?"

"Just as old as he is."

"How old?"

"He is sixty-six years old."

"How old are you, Mama?"

"I'm thirty-six."

"I'm three."

"Yes, I know."

"I'll be four in—" Louise's fingers danced "—six days."

Her mother nodded, acknowledging the correct answer while hoping to encourage silence, to no avail.

"Mary and Jeremy and Joseph and Charles and Nem are all older than me. Only John is younger. I like being older than somebody, but why can't we all be the same age?"

"Because I can grow only one of you inside me at a time."

"So we grow inside you like a potato or a turnip grows in the earth?"

"Something like that."

"Then am I a tuber or a taproot?"

"You are a precocious gift from God."

Louise frowned. "You mean precious."

"Do I?"

"Will you grow a younger sister for me?"

"If God so decides."

"When I am fully grown, I'll figure out how to fix Papa's eyes."

"That may not be so easy as you imagine."

"I'm very clever, Mama."

"Indeed you are, Louise. You're the most clever three-year-old I know."

"Can you imagine how clever I might be when I'm as old as you?"

"No, dear. I suspect I cannot."

———————✦———————

SUNDAY EVENING, 16 MARCH 1879
33 ORCHARD STREET
BRISTOL, ENGLAND

"And what of your family?" Louise asked Isabella.

Cheerily, Isabella said, "Doddy and Adeline are my family."

"Have you any brothers or sisters?"

"No, I'm afraid not."

"And what of your parents?" inquired Louise.

Lindsey broke the uncomfortable silence that followed. "They disowned her, due to the circumstances of our marriage."

As someone who made his living asking awkward questions, Lindsey seemed unflappable, but, with respect to Isabella, Louise thought she detected a blush rising on the cheeks beneath suddenly downcast lashes.

"I apologize," said Louise, "for venturing where I do not belong. I'm frequently too inquisitive for my own good. Let us speak of matters more pleasant, shall we? Other than Eastlake, who is your favorite writer?"

Isabella quickly looked up at Louise and offered a ladylike laugh, covering her mouth with fingertips. "You'll think me foolish," she said.

"I absolutely will not," said a smiling Louise. "It is more likely that you will think me foolish when I reveal my favorite author."

"And who might that be?"

"You must answer first."

"Alright," conceded Isabella, more interested in quickly learning of Louise's secret than hiding hers. "My favorite author, other than Eastlake, is Eastlake."

After but a moment in which Louise and Isabella stared at one another, with smiles growing on each of them, they broke into open laughter. Lindsey looked on in confusion.

"I don't understand."

The two women stopped laughing for a moment, looked at him briefly, looked at one another again, and then began their merriment anew.

"I don't understand," Lindsey repeated, more confused than before.

Louise was the first to compose herself sufficiently to explain.

"Your lovely wife's favorite author is Charles Eastlake, who wrote so wonderfully of fashion and design."

"That much I understand."

"Her favorite author other than Charles Eastlake is none other than Mr. Eastlake's own lovely wife, Elizabeth, who writes so wonderfully of art and travel."

"Oh," said David, with an insincere smile, not finding any great humor in the coincidence.

Louise and Isabella looked again at each other, genuine mirth quelled but shared in a glance.

"Now for your favorite author," pressed Isabella, with such a pretty blending of entreaty and command in her look that refusal was impossible.

"A. M Barnard," replied Louise, quickly and to the point.

Quiet fell over the room.

"You probably know her as Louisa May Alcott," added Louise.

"Oh," said an obviously disappointed Isabella. "Yes, *Little Women*, Meg, Jo, Beth and Amy. Then *Little Men*. Yes, quite pleasant stories, each of them."

"You disapprove?"

"No, no, of course not. Certainly not. I don't understand, though, why you believed I would think you foolish for identifying such a prosaic author as your favorite."

"She is actually quite a fascinating woman, I assure you. Born to transcendentalist parents, she spent part of her youth living in the failed utopian community of Fruitland. Home schooled by her father, she learned also at the hands of Ralph Waldo Emerson, Henry David Thoreau, Nathaniel Hawthorne, and Margaret Fuller. She was a staunch abolitionist, not surprisingly I suppose, since her parents once allowed their family home to be used as a station for the underground railway. She claims that she once found an escaped slave hiding in her stove. She served as a nurse during the civil war, only briefly though since she was soon struck down by typhoid, barely surviving that deadly infection. Oh, but I ramble on too much, as I am prone to do."

"No, no, please continue," pleaded Isabella. "I want to hear of her alter ego as A.M. Barnard."

"You'll be sorry for it, and so shall I, perhaps; I warn you beforehand that I can go too far in revealing my thoughts," said Louise, smiling, even while she knit her brows.

"Then please do."

"Since you insist. My namesake, Louisa May Alcott, is not quite the delicate person usually portrayed by her publishers and reporters. In an interview with another namesake, Louise Chandler Moulton, Louisa explained that she was half-persuaded that she consisted of a man's soul put, by some freak of nature, into a woman's body."

Louise realized instantly her faux pas, another instance in which she allowed her loose words to run in front of her more carefully considered thoughts. She pressed ahead, though, without missing a beat, so as to not highlight her indecorum.

"She found herself as interested in the grotesque aspects of humans as in the normal aspects, such as those she portrayed in *Little Women*. Since she dared not write of lurid subjects under her own name, she adopted the androgynous *nom de plume* of A.M. Barnard, just as the Brontë sisters wrote, at least initially, under the pseudonyms of Currer, Acton, and Ellis Bell.

From Isabella's facial expression, Louise realized she had captured Isabella's attention. But Louise noticed also in the countenance an impending sense of discomfort, perhaps even disapproval. With growing concern, and a decision to temper her words, Louise continued her exposition.

"As A.M. Barnard, Alcott wrote what she called her blood and thunder tales, those being her more sensational stories, among them *The Mummy's Curse*. In that adventure, Alcott wrote of a mummified sorceress, discovered by an Egyptologist who stole her possessions, who set the mummy herself ablaze, and who then suffered the mysterious death of both his friend and his new wife."

"Oh, my!" replied the startled hostess.

Louise pondered whether she should continue, deciding to do so only after the silence began to grow heavy.

"As Barnard, Alcott also wrote *Fatal Follies*, telling of a new bride and groom, each secretly believing the other to be suffering from the identical form of monomania, specifically wanting to murder the person he or she loves. Though both are wrong in their suspicions, both die as a result of them."

"Oh, my!" repeated Isabella, prompting another pause.

Louise decided that she should go no further. She realized also that she should definitely not mention her own interest the mysterious and the bizarre, her own compulsion to write of such matters. She decided instead to deflect the conversation to matters more normal, more civil.

"That is a gorgeous dress."

"This?" asked Isabella, returning instantly to equanimity.

She rose and slowly turned so that Louise could see the entirety of her black-and-blue-ribbed faille ensemble.

"We cannot afford Paris originals of course," said Isabella, "but I have found a skilled dressmaker who can recreate any design pictured in *Le Moniteur de la Mode*. I'm particularly fond of those by Jules David, but then who is not?"

"I know so little of fashion," said Louise. "However, I am certainly glad that the bustle has gone out of style."

"Alas," Isabella predicted, returning to her chair, "it will return, and with a fury, I fear. Your attire, if I may be so bold to say, is agreeably neat. I do so love green."

Louise's fingers played over her jacket's front. "I like its simplicity," she said. "And these many black buttons."

"I suspect Eastlake would find my apparel to be the more *handsome*," Isabella said, "for its ornamentation, and more *el-*

egant, for my tight corseting. All things considered, though, if he prefers his people as he prefers his furniture, he must hold in high esteem those who pretend to be nothing more or less than who they are. I sense that in you, Louise. I hope we will be friends."

Louise smiled and lifted her teacup. "To friendship."

chapter six
THE INQUEST

Sebastian Lilly was more than pleased to allow use of his hostelry for the inquest. This one seemed certain to return an indictment for murder, he thought, and would therefore be particularly profitable. The jurymen had already packed themselves shoulder-to-shoulder around three sides of a large table, each with a drink in front of him. Coroner Quinton Welch himself occupied the top of the table, facing the makeshift witness stand beyond. Other than three places reserved for and filled by the witnesses Dr. Daniel Weston, Detective John Reeves, and eyewitness Louise Hawkins, and a side seat for Welch's recording secretary, no other chairs could be found in the room. Better to squeeze in men with coin in their pockets, the innkeeper thought. Even with this arrangement and every room rented, potential patrons crowded the door, pressing in from the street beyond, each of them hoping for the slightest peek or overheard word. Men clustered in the stairway leading to the upper rooms, many with mugs in hand, or eating the pasties that Lilly had the foresight to order from the bakery. The Full Moon might take in a week's profit on this day alone.

Experienced in the nature of crowds and courts, David Lindsey and Jim Jeffers easily wedged their way through the compacted mass of humanity until they stood just inside the door, each with pencil and writing pad in hand. The horde of onlookers meant that there was not room enough for even a single camera. The constant commotion meant that there was no value in attempting to capture a still image. If the exposure time could somehow, in the future, be reduced to less than a second, thought Lindsey, then the camera might finally attain its ultimate worth.

John Hawkins and Mrs. Croton managed to place themselves no better than at the edge of the crowd that spilled out onto Broad Street. They could only hope for tidbits of information that might pass through the crowd like a vagrant breeze, likely shortened and mutated at every transfer.

Isabella Lindsey had sent her husband off that morning with a warm breakfast and warmer reassurances that she had no interest in being party to any such lewd and raucous gathering. Instead, she fretted briefly for Louise, then visited her seamstress. She felt there was nothing like a new dress to set the world right.

Coroner Welch was a short, spherical man with a too-small powdered wig, a ruffled shirt that fit like sausage casing, and a blue coat that had long ago given up the attempt to close around his burgeoning waistline. "Quiet yourselves all," he called, loudly enough to rouse the dead from their graves. The crowd obliged, eager as they were to hear every licentious detail.

"I am Mr. Quinton Welch, coroner for the County of the Town of Bristol. It has fallen upon me to faithfully and properly conduct this inquest into the death of Lt. William Perenna of Torquay Terrace in Clifton. The purpose of this inquest is, first and foremost, to ascertain truly the cause, place, and time of Lt. Perenna's death. It is rather for truth of the fact than it is for accusation. Nevertheless, an indictment may result."

Hoots and hollers erupted, not only from the crowd but also from several of the jurymen. Coroner Welch continued speaking above the din.

"On this account," he bellowed, somewhat quelling the crowd so he could continue in a more seemly tone, "it is my duty to receive evidence on oath, as well as on behalf of any party arrested or accused by the Crown. It is my intent to proceed apace and in accordance with all established law and custom. Never once has one of my inquests been quashed, and I intend that this will not be the first. The first rule of every inquest is that it must be taken *super visum corporis*, that is, within view of the body. I therefore this morning assembled you sixteen jurymen before me now, swore you to your oaths, then adjourned with you to the mortuary of the Central Station on Bridewell Street. Together, we viewed the body, as we are legally bound to do, and our viewing was duly recorded by my secretary, Mr. Fitzroy Smithers, seated now to my right."

Welch extended a fleshy hand to indicate a bespectacled and cadaverous man of perhaps thirty, or perhaps one hundred and thirty. Inexplicably, a few in the crowd cheered while others booed. Smithers offered no reaction to his sudden celebrity.

"In the presence of these same jurymen," continued Welch, unperturbed by the shouting, "I will now take the testimony of any person who can give evidence material to this inquest. As coroner, I have issued summonses for certain witnesses. All evidence must be given under the sanction of an oath, and shall be taken down with the greatest possible accuracy as to all material points of the inquiry. It is not possible that Mr. Smithers, quick as he is, shall adhere to every letter, syllable, or word, although even these he will not needlessly depart from. When no further evidence can be produced, it will become the province of you jurymen, and you alone, to consider and determine the facts of the case. You are neither to expect, nor should you be bound to any specific or direct opinion of mine regarding said facts."

Several jurymen thumped their mugs on the table to emphasize the point, pleased by the power they held. Welch quieted them again with his voice.

"But in questions of law, you jurymen ought always to show the most respectful deference to my advice and recommendation. Your verdict should be compounded of the facts as detailed to you by the witnesses, and of the law as I state it to you. If you jurymen are not unanimous, it shall be my duty to collect your voices and, provided twelve of you agree, to take the verdict according to the opinion of the majority. Now then, it may so happen that twelve of you cannot agree to abide by the majority. In such instance you will be kept without meat, drink, or fire until you return a verdict."

"We shall soon be eating and drinking heartily," laughed a ruddy and nearly sober juryman. "I can assure you of that."

The crowd broke out in uproarious laughter, and several jurymen struck the table with their palms and mugs. Outwardly, Welch ignored them. Inwardly, he wished for a large and sturdy gavel such as those allowed his American counterparts. Or an axe, he mused, then shook himself back to attention.

"Upon hearing your finding," he boomed, quieting the crowd again, "I shall draw up the inquisition, to which all of you and I must put our hands, and against which I must put my seal. This being done, no coroner, myself included, will have authority to hold a second inquisition upon this same matter unless this one first be quashed. As I have already mentioned, no inquest bearing my seal has ever been quashed. When the proceedings are closed, I will issue a warrant for the burial of William Perenna's body and, if appropriate, a warrant for any and all persons who may have been responsible for his death. As the first witness, I call Miss Louise Hawkins."

Louise rose and tried to hobble her way to the dock. The crowded conditions, however, left no clear pathway for Louise and her crutches. "Make way, make way!" ordered Welch, causing some jurors to skid closer to the central table, some of the citizenry to shuffle backwards, and members of the press to fill whatever void might have been made. "Make way," ordered Welch, "or I shall have you removed from the room."

Just as a gopher somehow tunnels through dirt, Louise managed to weave through the crowd. "Excuse me. Thank you," she said. "Careful there, don't step on the man behind you. Thank you, sir, very kind of you. That should do. Thank you, all." Eventually, she took her position in the makeshift witness stand, settled onto her crutches, and raised her right hand most of the way.

"Do you swear that the evidence which you shall give to this inquest on behalf of our Sovereign Lady the Queen, touching the death of William Perenna, shall be the truth, the whole truth, and nothing but the truth, so help you God?"

"I so swear to God," answered Louise.

"Miss Hawkins," he began, "I understand that you were the first to enter the house on Torquay Terrace after a gunshot was heard to come from within."

Louise, recognizing no question, gave no answer.

"Is that true?" pressed the coroner.

"It is," she answered.

"Please explain to these jurymen what you discovered upon entering that house."

"My attention was drawn first to a woman standing in the middle of a small room. I saw her in profile, facing to my left. She was obviously in a family way and wore an indecipherable look on her face."

"Excuse me, Miss Hawkins," interrupted the coroner. "Was the woman you saw the same woman now in custody at the Bristol Central Station?"

"I couldn't say, sir, since I have not talked to any person in custody at the Central Station. I can testify that the woman of whom I speak was in the presence of the police while I was still in that room. They insisted I leave, though I wanted to remain and comfort her. The constable who took charge informed me that they would take care of the woman, and I had no choice but to take him at his word."

"Do you know if the woman you saw is Anna Perenna?"

"That is what I read in the newspapers, sir, but I have no direct knowledge of that."

"Detective Reeves," said the coroner, shifting in his seat, "I am now going to place you under oath. There is no need for you to take the stand. Simply rise where you are. Do you swear that the evidence which you shall give to this inquest on behalf of our Sovereign Lady the Queen, touching the death of William Perenna, shall be the truth, the whole truth, and nothing but the truth, so help you God?"

"I do," said the detective after standing and raising his right hand.

"Now, Detective Reeves, can you confirm that the woman removed from the house at 22 Torquay Terrace is the same woman now in custody at the Central Station?"

"I can," said the detective.

"Can you confirm that she goes by the name Anna Perenna?"

"She has said not a word since her arrest, sir. However, we have spoken with her neighbors, who confirmed without exception that she does in fact go by the name of Anna Perenna and is, or was, the wife of the victim, William Perenna."

"Thank you, Detective. You may be seated. Please continue, Miss Hawkins."

"Because of her gaze," Louise continued, "my attention was drawn to the wall on my left. There I witnessed a large splash of blood and brain matter, beneath which ran a bloody smear leading to the head of the victim." Murmuring spread among the crowd, none of whom had ever heard a woman use the term *brain matter* before, even in private, much less in public.

"Excuse me once again, Miss Hawkins," said Welch. "Can you confirm whether that victim went by the name of William Perenna?"

"I cannot."

He sighed. "Detective, can you confirm that the victim found in the house on Torquay Terrace was William Perenna?"

Detective Reeves popped to his feet. "We can, sir. He was known directly by several constables in our department, and the neighbors identified him as such."

"Thank you, Detective. Be seated. You may continue, Miss Hawkins."

"William Perenna, as he is now known to me, was lying almost entirely on his back. Only his head was not on the floor but instead inclined against the wall, with his neck bent at nearly ninety degrees. It seemed to me that blood coming from the back of his head made the streaks down the wall as his feet slid out from beneath him. As I entered, blood continued to flow from the back of his head, pooling beneath him. He had suffered a terrible wound to his forehead, and was clearly dead of that wound."

"We'll hear from Dr. Weston on that point, Miss Hawkins. Did you witness a gun in the room?"

"Yes, sir. There was a revolver on the floor between the wife and the husband."

"Can you be more precise regarding the position of this weapon?"

"Yes." There was an expectant pause.

"Then please be so," Welch grumbled.

"The revolver was approximately four feet forward of where Anna Perenna stood, approximately two feet from the stocking feet of William Perenna, where he sprawled on the floor."

"Detective Reeves, please show us the revolver recovered from the house. Miss Hawkins, can you confirm that this is the weapon you saw?"

"It appears to be the same weapon, sir, but I only had a glance of it at the scene. Since many revolvers look nearly identical, I cannot confirm that the revolver in the detective's hand is the same one that was on the floor of the house on Torquay Terrace."

"Detective, can you confirm that is the same weapon the police removed from the house at 22 Torquay Terrace on the day of the shooting there?"

"Yes, sir," Reeves said. "A constable recovered this Colt Navy revolver from beneath a couch. The Bristol Police have maintained possession of it ever since."

"Miss Hawkins, do you know how this weapon came to be moved from the position you described to its location under the couch, whence the police recovered it?"

"Yes."

The coroner chafed that Louise again answered a question without automatically expanding on her answer. "Then please explain that to these jurymen."

"Anna Perenna seemed on the verge of fainting, thus I entered the room to steady her, but nearly fell myself, due to my recently sprained ankle. My brother John, therefore, stepped forward and escorted her to a divan to my right. I joined her there and tried to console her."

Boos and hisses could be heard from the crowd. "Please continue," said Welch, after waving the crowd to silence.

"John went to quiet a sounding teapot. Two newspapermen then intruded with cameras. One trained his camera on the victim, the other on Anna Perenna and myself. She screamed, which alerted my brother who, ah, interrupted that second photographer. In the scuffle that followed, one of them, I know not which, kicked the revolver under the divan."

"So the location of the revolver, as the police discovered it beneath the divan, is of no importance with respect to who may have shot William Perenna?"

"No, sir, not that I can imagine," Louise responded.

"Very well. When you first entered the house, did you see any person within it, other than William and Anna Perenna?"

"No, sir."

"Did you see any person flee from the house before you entered?"

"No, sir."

"When you first heard the gunshot, were you in a position to notice anyone leaving the house, if one had done so?"

"Had anyone fled via the front of the house, after the gunshot but before my arrival, I would have seen that person."

"Could someone have left the back way without you knowing of it?"

"Yes, sir."

"Detective, what do you say to this?"

Detective Reeves stood. "There is a door at the back of the house, sir, and the constable first on the scene confirmed to me that the door was locked from within, as were the windows."

"Thank you, Detective," said the coroner. "Thank you, Miss Hawkins. I have no further questions for you, however some of the jurymen might."

"Indeed I do," said one of the jurymen.

"Proceed, Mr, ah—" the coroner consulted the list of names thrust forward by his secretary "—Mr. Caggs."

The hirsute gentleman smoothed his vest and cleared his throat before addressing Louise. "Madam, I read the newspapers, same as you. I heard your description of what you witnessed, but not a thing about her confession. Why is that? Do you sympathize with the woman, despite her licentious behavior while her husband served Queen and country abroad, despite even her murdering him upon his return?"

"You ask two questions, sir," replied Louise evenly. "Ask me one and I shall answer it."

Juryman Caggs, narrowing his eyes at Louise's lack of respect for his position, narrowed his questioning. "Why is it, then, that you said nothing of her confession?"

"I was not asked about a confession," Louise replied, "so I did not answer about a confession."

"But you heard her confess?" Caggs pressed.

"No sir, I heard no one confess to the shooting, or to any other offense."

"She was begging for mercy, was she not?"

"Not once in my presence did Anna Perenna ever beg for mercy."

"Are you telling me that the newspapers, all of them, are wrong?"

"I cannot speak to all of the newspapers, sir, since I have not read them all, but most newspapers are wrong most of the time." A ripple of laughter spread through the room, the reporters most amused of all. Caggs, however, scowled.

"I have this with me," he said. "It's the *Clifton Chronicle*, and its headline reads, 'Soon-to-be Mother Confesses to Murder.' And here, several lines into the story, it mentions you, I believe: 'Even before the police arrived, a neighbor discovered the pistol at her feet. The murderess was weeping and begging forgiveness for shooting her husband.' What do you say to that?"

"I have not been summoned here to testify to the accuracy or inaccuracy of the *Clifton Chronicle*. I have been summoned to answer questions about what I know of the shooting on Torquay Terrace."

"Was the woman you saw in the room weeping?"

"Yes, she was."

"Was she begging forgiveness?"

"Yes."

"Well, that equates to a confession," Caggs sniffed.

"No, it does not."

"Well, it does to me."

Several of his fellows beat on the table in support. Halfheartedly, Welch ordered them to silence before asking,

"Does any other juryman have a question of this witness?"

None did.

"Does anyone in the *room* have a question of this witness?" he asked, sounding half-asleep.

"Who's the father?" came a drunken shout from near the doorway, to the merriment of almost everyone in earshot.

"*That* is an improper question," said the coroner with a hint of a grin. "The citizenry may ask questions, but the questions must be pertinent to the death of William Perenna or any person who may be responsible for his death. Does anyone have a pertinent question?"

"I do," shouted a different voice inside the inn. "Who's the father?"

Laughter burst forth, prompting only a shaking of the head by the coroner.

"You may step down, Miss Hawkins," he intoned over the tittering and guffawing that still permeated the room. "As the next witness, I call Dr. Daniel Weston."

Louise somehow managed to regain her chair as the crowd stilled for the esteemed Dr. Weston, rising to his full six feet. Adorned in a frock coat, he left his silk-lined bowler hat on his chair, exposing his full crop of sandy, wavy, pomaded hair for all to admire. He stepped up with an air of justified confidence and, upon taking the stand, removed a pair of badly scratched, folding pince-nez spectacles from his coat pocket, then perched them in precarious fashion on his nose. Perhaps out of respect for his polished mien, the spectacles teetered not one degree as the doctor offered his testimony, which consisted almost entirely of reading his own autopsy report into the record. Louise noted his omission of William Perenna's syphilitic chancre.

After Dr. Weston's reading, the coroner placed the jurymen under the charge of his secretary. "Mr. Smithers, you shall well and truly keep the jury upon this inquiry without meat, drink, or fire. You shall not suffer any person to speak to them, nor shall you speak to them yourself, unless it is to ask them if they have agreed on their verdict, until they shall be agreed. So help you God."

"So help me God," swore the secretary, before escorting the jurymen to a side room and locking them in.

The jurymen's raucous laughter was easily heard through the door that supposedly gave them privacy. Their merry deliberations quickly led to a unanimous verdict against Anna Perenna for murder. It took them less than eight minutes. The crowd cheered and Welch made no effort to call them to order. All that remained was for him to sign the paperwork that, in an act of prescience, he had filled out the previous evening. After signing the two critical documents, he declared his inquest to be closed, then modestly received the accolades of his admiring public before leading them to the bar, where Sebastian Lilly already busied himself, pouring the patrons of the Full Moon mug after mug of ale and port, each delivered with a solicitous grin.

Quinton Welch's indictment read:

> An inquisition taken for our Sovereign Lady the Queen, taken at the house commonly called or known by the name of Full Moon Inn and Tavern, situated along Broad Street in the Town of Bristol, in the County of the Town of Bristol, England, on the seventeenth day of March, in the forty-first year of the reign of our Sovereign Lady Victoria, before Quinton Welch, Gentleman, one of the Coroners of our said Lady the Queen for the said County, on view of the body of William Perenna, then and there lying dead, upon the oath and affirmation of:
> Dwennon Battons of Clifton,
> Brandon Hepworth of Stoke Gifford,
> Landon Fang of Clifton,
> Nash Stryver of Filton,
> Chilton Darnay of Avonmouth,
> Brinley Barlow of Frampton Cotterell,
> Denton Grannett of Cotham,
> Keyon Wackles of Patchway,
> Beldon Orlick of Mangotsfield,
> Ewing Mould of Winterborne,

> *Waverly Glubb of Filton,*
> *Wright Limbkins of Avonmouth,*
> *Ackley Sparsit of Almondsbury,*
> *Alvin Fizkin of Bristol,*
> *Elmer Caggs of Patchway, and*
> *Dempster Herring of Filton,*

all good and lawful men of the said County, duly chosen, and who being then and there duly sworn and charged to inquire for our said Lady the Queen, when, how, and by what means the said William Perenna came to his death, do upon their oaths say that on the thirteenth day of March, in the year aforesaid, one Anna Perenna, feloniously, wilfully, and of her malice aforethought, did Kill and Murder William Perenna by shooting him in the head, against the peace of our Lady the Queen, her Crown and Dignity. In witness whereof, the said Coroner and the Jurors aforesaid have hereunto set and subscribed their hands the day and year first above written.

> *Quinton Welch, Coroner*

His warrant read:

> *To the keeper of Her Majesty's Jail of Bristol, a Warrant for Detention, to wit—*
> *Whereas you have in your custody the person of Anna Perenna; and whereas by an Inquisition taken before me, one of Her Majesty's Coroners for the said County of the day and year hereunder written, in the County of the Town of Bristol, on view of the body of William Perenna, then and there lying dead, she, the said Anna Perenna, stands charged with the wilful Murder of the said William Perenna. Therefore in Her Majesty's name, by virtue of my Office, I charge and command you to detain and keep in your custody the person of the said Anna Perenna until she shall be thence discharged by due Course of Law; and for your so doing this is your Warrant.*

Given under my hand and Seal this seventeenth day of March, of the year one thousand eight hundred and seventy-nine,
        Quinton Welch, Coroner

chapter seven

THE RECREATION

Upper Swandam Lane was little more than a rank alley running behind the houses on Torquay Terrace, an unexpectedly grim place, given the fine homes it backed. Only an ivied wall chest-high to John Hawkins separated Louise, John, and Lindsey from the house where William Perenna had recently met his fate. The trio scouted the alley to ensure they were unobserved, and then inartfully clambered over the wall. Louise, who had thrown her purse and crutches to the far side, received a boost from John, the last to cross over, and an assist from Lindsey, the first to gain the other side. In the process, she snagged and ripped her dress. Looking at the small tear, she sighed, "Drat," recovered her purse and crutches, followed the others to the rear door of the house, and examined the lock.

"It's not a Bramah, not even a Chubb," she whispered. "I should have no difficulty opening it."

From her purse, she extracted a handkerchief containing several lock picking tools, selected a slender torsion wrench and a hook pick, inserted them into the keyhole, and manipulated them until she heard a faint click. She turned the handle. The door opened.

"Remarkable," exclaimed Lindsey, as they entered the house.

"*The Construction of Locks*," said Louise, as if the book was common reading in everyone's household. "You should read it. It's a collection of papers written by none other than Alfred

Charles Hobbs, that clever American who managed to first pick a Chubb lock, then to pick even a Bramah, as a demonstration at London's Great Exhibition of fifty-one. One might as well learn from the master."

"How *do* you find the time?" asked Lindsey.

"How can I *not* pursue such fascinating subjects? As a lady, I am not supposed to be interested in such matters, but I absolutely abhor dull, routine existence. I depend on the unusual aspects of life to fend off ennui. I suspect, sir, you know of what I speak."

Louise quickly made her way through the kitchen, leaving Lindsey little time to ponder the depth of her observation. Instead, he followed her down the passageway to and into the front room, John lagging only slightly. There, each of the three stood and stared at the dried splotch on the wall, time having dulled it from scarlet to brown. Streaks still led downward to the large stain on the floor.

Louise whipped her magnifying glass from her purse, then set her purse on the floor and approached the bloodstained wall. Though hindered by her bandaged foot, her slight stature, and her intent to avoid the stain on the floor, she carefully examined the splash on the wall. Standing on one tiptoe, she used the glass to examine the bullet hole punctuating the middle of the splash, making inaudible comments to herself in the process. This done, she followed the markings that led down the wall until she could bend no further. Then, to Lindsey's amazement, she laid herself flat on the floor, parallel to the wall, holding the magnifying glass just inches from the dried blood that had earlier pooled there.

"My hook pick, please, John," she said without diverting her attention from the blood, "and tweezers."

Having never held hers or any woman's purse before, John was surprised by how heavy it was. He dropped his hand inside expecting to easily find the desired objects by feel, thus preserving Louise's privacy as much as possible, but soon recognized the futility of the tactile approach. Only then did he look inside. He found a veritable treasury of coins; multiple handkerchiefs; a pair of gloves that he had never seen her wear; several unmentionables; a bottle of laudanum; a pocket edition of Boccaccio's *Decameron*; a collapsing ruler; a silver ladies' watch of conventional design and a substantially larger one with two stem winders; two unsealed letters, each in a man's handwriting, and a telegram, folded closed; a decorative pin in the shape of a bulldog's head, with ruby eyes; a ring bearing a Masonic device; two long hairpins; and, finally, a confusing array of slender metal tools, the specific purposes of which John could only begin to guess. Focusing on the tools and rummaging through them, he managed to find the tweezers and the hook pick, recognizing the second item only for having just seen his sister use it to gain their entry.

"Eureka!" he exclaimed triumphantly, dropping the purse with a clunk before placing the tools in his sister's outstretched hand.

"Thank you, John. Now please step back and allow me as much light as possible."

With the hook pick, she scraped at the residual blood here and there, dissatisfied with the results. Finally she murmured, "Hello, hello, hello! What's this?" She tweezed something invisible to John and Lindsey, and examined the mysterious item by rotating her hand, flexing her wrist, and inspecting it from every angle.

She then eased her body away from the wall, scouring the floor every inch of the way. So engrossed was she with her occupation that she appeared to have forgotten the presence of her companions, for she chattered away under her breath the whole time, keeping up a running narrative of exclamations, groans, whistles, and little cries suggestive of encouragement and of hope. As Lindsey watched her, he was irresistibly reminded of a pureblooded, well-trained foxhound whining in its eagerness when it comes across the lost scent. For five minutes or more she continued her researches, scrutinizing each scrap she plucked from the floor.

"They say that genius is an infinite capacity for taking pains," she finally remarked, wobbling to her feet and reclaiming her crutches. "It's a very bad definition, but it does apply to detective work."

"What have you discovered?" asked Lindsey.

"I know exactly where William Perenna was standing when he was shot, a critical fact in our impending calculations. I already knew Anna Perenna's position, since I discovered her standing here," Louise said, vaulting on her crutches and turning to face the wall. "There's no evidence on the floor indicating that she moved to this spot after the gunshot. There was little time for her to do so in any case. Therefore, I think it's safe to conclude that she did not move during the interval between the gunshot and my arrival. William Perenna was standing there, in his stocking feet, facing his wife, his heels twelve inches from the wall."

"How can you possibly know that?" asked Lindsey, shaking his head in wonder as John watched his sister proudly.

"Every contact leaves a trace," she replied. "Wherever anyone steps, whatever anyone touches, he leaves something of himself that serves as silent witness of his actions. Not only his fingerprints or his footprints, but also his hair, skin, sweat, and blood—even fibers from his clothes. This physical evidence does not forget, nor is it ever confused by the excitement of the moment. Eyewitness evidence is fallible in the extreme, but physical evidence cannot possibly be wrong. It can never perjure itself. It might certainly be overlooked, and it can be terribly misinterpreted, but it cannot, at its core, be wrong. Only human failure to find it, to study and understand it, without bias or prejudice, can ever diminish its value."

"And what did you find?" asked John.

"Wool fibers, John, clean and fresh from Lt. Perenna's socks, the very socks he was wearing, possibly for the first time in his life, certainly the last. He must have purchased them recently, as a kindness to his wife. Imagine, if you dare, the state of a soldier's socks, first thing off a troopship. Feet perspire more than any other part of the body, up to a pint a day, but the Lieutenant's socks were reasonably fresh and showed no sign of fraying or wearing from repeated use."

"And how do the threads you found identify the location where he was standing when shot?"

"It seemed clear to me, immediately on first viewing the scene, that his feet had slid away from the wall as his head slid down it. Had he been wearing his boots, his feet would not have slid from beneath him, he would have crumpled in place. I suspected that some fibers from his socks must have been snagged by small irregularities in the wooden floor, hence my search for them. I found the first a foot from the wall, the last just about where I remember his feet having come to rest."

"Remarkable," exclaimed Lindsey. "If you had been born earlier, they would have burned you as a necromancer."

"She was standing right here when I first saw her," said Louise, ignoring Lindsey's strange compliment. "The revolver was there, four feet in front of her." She indicated a point on the floor. "Mr. Lindsey, measure the distance to the wall, please."

Lindsey pulled open his measuring tape and placed its lead end near Louise's feet. With one crutch, she pinned it down. Lindsey backed towards the wall, the flat steel band unreeling along the floor.

"I'm sinfully envious of your Chesterman tape measure," Louise observed. "Such a fine instrument is far too dear for the limits of my meager annuity."

"I'll bequeath this one to you," replied Lindsey, from a short distance away, "in case Isabella ever shoots me in the forehead. Eleven feet, two inches between your toes and the wall."

"One hundred and thirty-four inches," Louise interrupted. "So the revolver would have been eighty-six inches from the wall. The autopsy report says that William Perenna was six feet tall. That's seventy-two inches. Most of him lay on the floor. Only his head rested against the wall. Leonardo's *Vitruvian Man* shows a man's head is one eighth of his height, placing Lt. Perenna's feet approximately sixty-three inches from the wall. The revolver was therefore approximately twenty-three inches from his feet, forty-eight from hers. That's a ratio of nearly one to two, just as I visualized that day. Now for the height of the bullet hole from the floor."

She caught the dying sound of John's woeful, barely audible moan, and turned. Struck by his appearance, she felt a surge of guilt sweep over her. She had paid too little attention to his needs ever since the shooting, even while he had been so gallant with her.

"You shouldn't have ventured out today, John," she said gently. "Not with your ague flaring up."

"And you shouldn't be roaming God's creation with your maimed ankle," he replied, wincing and while wiping his brow, "but here we are."

"I wish you had not delayed your move to Ventnor," she said, suddenly rueful. "You know that I'll miss you terribly when you go, but you must have that clean Channel air. Even here in Clifton the air has not been as helpful as we hoped."

"I'll be gone soon enough." The words hung heavy, leaving Louise with the clear understanding that the subject was not to be raised again. "Mr. Lindsey, please, the distance from the floor to the bullet hole."

Lindsey placed the lead of the measuring tape at the base of the wall, and, holding it there with his toe, measured the distance up the wall to the small hole in the center of the splash. "Five feet, nine inches."

"That makes sense," said Louise. "The lieutenant was six feet tall and the exit wound was three inches from the top of his head. Let's try this." She turned back to Lindsey. "I'll remain here, where Anna stood, and you stand where William must have been standing, your heels twelve inches from the wall. A bit closer—yes, right there. And you need to somehow be a foot taller."

"Ten inches," said Lindsey, earnestly.

"As you say," allowed Louise. "John, can you make him ten inches taller?"

John, assessing the situation, retrieved from the kitchen two of the largest pots available and placed them upside-down in the spot Lindsey vacated, forming two ten-inch-tall platforms. When Lindsey moved to step up on them, John interceded: "Hold on. Neither is quite ten inches." John rounded up two thick books and two issues of *Cornhill Magazine*, setting them on the overturned pots. Lindsey dropped the Chesterman into John's waiting hand, and John used the tape to measure the height of each stack. "An eighth inch shy on the left, a quarter on the right."

"Close enough, for our work, certainly. Nicely done, John. Now, Mr. Lindsey, if you will be so kind as to grow ten inches."

Lindsey, steadying himself with one hand on John's shoulder, dared to mount the precarious platforms.

"Is the center of his forehead," asked Louise of John, "now aligned with the bullet hole in the wall?"

John craned his neck. "It seems to be."

"Now, John, assuming that Mr. Lindsey can do without you," she said, prompting Lindsey to lift his hand from John's shoulder, "perhaps you could help me grow two inches, so I might be as tall as Anna Perenna."

Leaving Lindsey's side, John selected another book and a house wares catalog, each about an inch thick, and stacked them just beside Louise's left foot. He grasped her, from behind, by her waist, to aid her ascent. Atop the books, she performed her own balancing act. Dropping the left crutch and steadying herself with the right one, she raised her left arm and pointed her index finger at Lindsey's forehead, as if aiming a revolver. John stood nearby, planning to catch her should she fall, but she had another assignment for him.

"We ought to hurry," she said, increasingly excited by the developing trigonometry. "Measure the length from the floor to my shoulder. That's the last measurement we need. I cannot hold myself here much longer." Her exhilaration and unsteadiness increased in parallel as John recovered the Chesterman to measure the distance from the floor to Louise's left shoulder.

"Fifty-one and seven eighths of an inch," he announced, just as Louise toppled, slightly backwards but mostly sideward, towards her brother, who moved to catch her but lost his own balance in the process. Both of them tumbled to the ground, she landing on top. The Chesterman escaped during the fall and skittered across the floor as its metal tape automatically retracted. It clanged against one of Lindsey's pots, prompting him to take a quick but imprudent step forward, which brought the collapse of the tenuous platforms and sent him also to the ground, even as he yelled to Louise, "Take care!"

Cushioned by both John and her petticoats, Louise was indeed unhurt, at least seriously, as evidenced by the dexterity with which she rolled off John and the speed of her hands-and-knees crawl towards her purse. She scampered, four-limbed, while proclaiming, "You saw it yourselves! You saw it! No need to await my calculations. It's obvious, isn't it?"

John and Lindsey looked on as she gained her purse, and withdrew the bizarrely complex watch-like device that John had encountered during his earlier rummaging. She assumed a sitting position, legs crossed, her modesty protected only by layers and layers of undergarments. She focused on her device as she alternately turned its two different stems. Confused beyond words, the two uninjured gentlemen rose to stand over her and study her actions.

"It's not a watch," crowed Lindsey, recognizing the four concentric rings of numbers orbiting the device's center. "It's a Boucher Calculator!"

SIXTEEN YEARS EARLIER
SATURDAY MORNING, 1 MARCH 1863
SOUTHFIELD COTTAGE, LECKHAMPTON ROAD
LECKHAMPTON, ENGLAND

"A happy unbirthday to you, Jeremy," said five-year-old Louise Hawkins to her brother.

Jeremy had been born fifteen years earlier, on the twenty-ninth of February. His birthday appeared only during years evenly divisible by four, except on century years. But he would never see a century year.

"Oh, bother!" he said, with mock concern. "You've been reading *Through the Looking Glass*. There will be no end to your allusions now. I recall what happened after you read *Alice in Wonderland*."

"May I examine your unbirthday present?" she asked, with all seriousness.

Jeremy handed her his new slide rule. She studied it.

"Elliott Brothers," she read. "449 Strand. It's boxwood. Just like your old one, except this one is new so its little tics are still dark. Oh, and it slides smoothly—much nicer than your old one. It's beautiful. A happy unbirthday to you indeed, dear brother."

"Turn it over," said Jeremy. "Look at the back."

Louise did, and gasped at what she saw. "Oh, my! These scales are new. Your old one was simply blank. You'll now do calculations far beyond me. What are they? Tell me! What can they do?"

"Trigonometry and logarithms," he replied, delighted by her exuberance.

"Show me!"

"It's too soon. You must continue your studies until you understand trigonometry and logarithms, then you will be ready for such a grand calculating device. Perhaps mother will give you one of your own."

Her shoulders slumped. She passed the slide rule back to her brother, who set it on his roll top desk.

"Your birthday is just forty days from now. You'll be six, I believe," he said, as if he wasn't sure, "and you are already skilled at multiplication and division, with a beginner's understanding of algebra. Those are most impressive for one so young."

"But I want to be skilled at trigonometry and logarithms," she said, disheartened.

"Patience is a virtue, Louise."

"Patience only means 'no, not today.'"

"Well," said Jeremy, "as you have just taught me, the best gifts need not be held until a birthday." He pulled open the drawer, withdrew his old slide rule, and handed it to her.

"Happy unbirthday to you, beloved sister."

Thrilled almost beyond words, she stared at her new slide rule as if it were a crown jewel, and then cradled it as if it were a baby doll. "Thank you, Jeremy! Oh, thank you so much, more than I can say. It's the best unbirthday gift I've ever received."

"Many happy calculations to you," said Jeremy, turning back to his work, struck suddenly by a stray thought. No need for a slide rule to be long. It could be circular, then it could fit in a pocket. Maybe someday she would own a circular slide rule.

Perhaps he would even be the one to give it to her, and be graced with that smile once again.

Tuesday morning, 18 March 1879
22 Torquay Terrace
Clifton, England

Louise stopped working her Boucher. "I need to calm down," she told herself, "and calculate it correctly this time. It is so very simple, yet I did it wrong." She took a deep breath before talking herself through the process. "The triangle of interest spanned from my shoulder to Lindsey, running parallel to the floor, then up to his forehead, then back to my shoulder."

"I'll trade you my Chesterman for that Boucher," offered Lindsey.

Louise was too focused on her calculation to note Lindsey's offer. "I want to calculate the angle of my arm above the horizontal," she mused.

"Plus a pound," said Lindsey, upping his offer. "My Chesterman plus a pound."

"That angle is the arctangent of the rise over the run."

"Two pounds."

"The rise," she continued, ignoring Lindsey's one-man auction, "is equal to the height of Lindsey's forehead minus the height of my shoulder, which is—seventeen and one eighth inches."

"My Chesterman and one of my Warren chairs—the one you liked so much."

"The run is twelve less than one hundred and thirty-four. So I set one to the index line," she said, turning the winder, "the needle to one two two. Rotate to one seven one two five. Aha! Mr. Lindsey, here's the most marvelous part of this calculation, and you may keep your chairs and cash and Chesterman, thank you, for this device means far too much to me. Look! I needn't even read the quotient off on front face. I can simply turn the calculator around, examine the innermost scale of the back face, and the desired angle is right there beneath the pointer line. See? Eight degrees."

She announced this gleefully, showing the calculator's reverse to Lindsey, then to John, then again to Lindsey.

"Jeremy recognized it immediately," she said, clearly in admiration of his spatial prescience. "He knew it even as he told us to come here and do the trigonometry ourselves. I failed to realize it until I pointed my finger at Mr. Lindsey's forehead. The precise angle is unimportant, but I simply could not keep myself from calculating it. It was eight degrees, but it could have just as well been five or ten or twenty. You saw it with your own eyes, not now, not looking at the reading on my calculator. You both saw it during our recreation. You just don't realize what was staring each of us in the face."

"What?" pleaded John. "What did we see?"

"That Anna Perenna could not have shot her husband."

And the small room fell silent.

chapter eight
A SHOOTING AT THE THREE CRIPPLES PUBLIC HOUSE

Tuesday evening, 18 March 1879
Three Cripples Public House
Bristol, England

God had once again called upon him to remove a gobbet of evil from the earth. It was his duty to scour the Easton suburb in search of that gobbet. God would tell him when he had found the right one. God had already identified the manner of removal to be used.

The filthy and miserable appearance of the neighborhood could hardly be imagined by any decent man who had not witnessed it. Wretched houses with broken windows patched with rags and paper; every room let out to a different family, and in many instances to two or even three families, or a dozen unrelated laborers; fruit and sweet-stuff manufacturers in the cellars, barbers and red-herring vendors in the front parlors, cobblers in the back; a bird-fancier in the first floor, three families on the second. Starvation in the attics, Irishmen in the passage, a musician in the front kitchen, and a charwoman and five hungry children in the back one. Filth everywhere; a gutter before the houses and a drain behind; clothes drying and slops emptied from the windows. Girls of fourteen or fifteen, with matted hair, walked about barefoot in grimy white greatcoats that were almost their only covering. Boys of all ages, in coats of all sizes and no coats at all. Men and women, in every variety of scanty and dirty apparel, lounging, scolding, drinking, smoking, squabbling, fighting, and swearing.

But at the very edge of the neighborhood, when he turned the corner, what a change! The Three Cripples public house, catering to both those beyond with a bit of money to spare, and those behind with no more than a coin or two, and that better spent elsewhere. It was all light and brilliancy, the Three Cripples. The hum of many voices issued from the gin shop with its fantastically ornamented parapet, with an illuminated clock, plate glass windows surrounded by stucco rosettes, and a profusion of gaslights in richly gilt burners. It was perfectly dazzling when contrasted with the darkness and dirt just behind.

He knew he would find his quarry within.

The interior was even gayer than the exterior. Beyond the parlor was a bar of French-polished mahogany, elegantly carved, along one wall and extending half the length of the room. Along the opposite wall were great casks, painted green and gold, bearing such inscriptions, as "Old Tom, 549," "Young Tom, 360," and 'Samson, 1421."

At the back of the barroom was a lofty and spacious saloon, full of the same enticing vessels. On the counter, in addition to the usual spirit apparatus, were two or three little baskets of cakes and biscuits, carefully secured at the top with wickerwork to prevent their contents from being unlawfully abstracted. Working the bar was the ostensible proprietor of the concern, a stout, coarse fellow in a fur cap put on very much to one side to give him a knowing air, and to display his sandy whiskers to the best advantage. Two shamefully dressed damsels, with large necklaces and larger bosoms, dispensed the food and spirits. One approached him, as he settled into an empty chair near the entry, but he waved her away. Instead of imbibing, as would be his normal and preferred practice, he scanned those who were already drinking. More particularly, he scanned those who had too long been drinking, searching for the man God had sent him to kill.

It didn't take him long. There, just three tables away, sat a man in a velveteen coat, drab shorts, half boots and stockings, brooding over a little pewter measure and a small glass. At his feet sat a white-coated, red-eyed dog who occupied himself, alternately, in winking at his master with both eyes and whining, almost imperceptibly, for a bit of food.

"Quiet, ya mangy varmint! Keep quiet!" said the man, suddenly breaking silence. Whether his meditations were so intense as to be disturbed by the dog's winking, or whether his feelings were so wrought upon that they required whatever relief derivable from attacking an unoffending animal, the effect was a kick and a curse bestowed simultaneously upon the dog.

Dogs are not generally apt to revenge injuries inflicted upon them by their masters, but the dog, having similar temperament as his owner, made no more ado but at once fixed his teeth in one of the boots. Having given the boot a hearty shake, the dog retired, growling, under a table, just escaping the pewter measure leveled at his head.

"You would, would ya?" shouted the dog's owner, poking at it with his cane in one hand, opening with the other a large clasp knife, quickly and expertly drawn from his pocket. "Come here, you born devil! Come here! D'ya hear?"

The dog no doubt heard, because his owner spoke in the harshest key of a harsh voice. The dog, however, remained where he was, growling more fiercely than before, grasping the end of the cane between his teeth, biting at it like a wild beast. This resistance only more infuriated the owner who, dropping on his knees, began to assail the animal most furiously. The dog jumped from right to left, and from left to right, snapping, growling, and barking. The man thrust and swore, and struck and blasphemed. The struggle was reaching a critical point for one or other when the outer door suddenly opened. The dog darted past the entering patron, leaving the owner on the floor, beneath a table, a cane and clasp knife in his hands.

"Damn dog!" he shouted, regaining his feet, chugging his drink and thrusting the remainder of his meal into his pocket. "Damn dog!" he repeated, as he made his way towards the rear stairway leading to the rooms above.

"Thank you, Lord," said the quiet man sitting by the entry door, almost to himself. "Thy Kingdom comes. Thy Will be done."

After waiting slightly more than a minute, he rose and walked to the bar, gained the proprietor's attention, and spoke to him in normal tone.

"I'd like to talk to that man about his dog. Which room does he occupy?"

"I'd like the both of 'em to keep the hell out of my establishment, but at least the man pays rent."

"The room number?"

"And I'd like you to buy some food or drink, rather than just sitting comfortably, soaking up my light and heat, asking questions for free."

"An ale and a cake, then."

"That'll be six pence."

The customer pulled a shilling from his pocket and dropped it onto the counter.

"That'll be room three, then," said the proprietor, replacing the shilling with six pence.

"I'll take my food and drink when I return," the customer said, pocketing the coins. He turned and began walking towards the stairs. "I won't be long," he added over his shoulder, not caring if anyone could hear him.

Room three was the second on the right. He entered without knocking. The dog owner-of-late was sitting on the edge of the bed, finishing his meal, a hunk of mutton hanging from his mouth. Surprised and angry by the sudden intrusion, he jumped to his feet and yelled, as best he could through the mouthful, "What the hell!"

The intruder calmly reached into his pocket, pulled forth a revolver, lifted it, stepped forward, and shot the man square in the forehead. The dead man fell back onto the bed, the mutton hunk falling from his gaping mouth and hitting the floor.

The quiet man returned the pistol to his pocket, and then pulled the dead man's boots from his feet, placing them neatly by the doorway.

A gigantic sense of relief, almost an ecstasy, washed over him. That sense of elation, however, was followed almost immediately by a tinge of disappointment, as it always was. "Am

I done now, Lord?" he asked, staring at the floor rather than towards Heaven. "Am I finally done?"

He waited, but no answer was forthcoming. It would be the last, he vowed, as he always vowed. But this one, it would indeed be his last. He walked from the room, closing the door behind him. He walked down the stairway, across the parlor, and to the bar. Everyone stared at him in quiet awe and wonderment. He took off his hat and wiped his forehead with his sleeve. He returned his hat, and pulled it tightly down over his head. He took a gulp of his ale and stuffed the cake into his pocket. He walked out the door.

As he expected, as he hoped, the dog was waiting there. He pulled the cake from his pocket and gave it to the scrawny dog, who wolfed it. He petted the animal on its head, and stroked its back twice, from head to tail. He then calmly disappeared into the squalid neighborhood whence he came, knowing that the police would not be patrolling amongst the wretchedly poor.

The dog followed him.

———※———

TUESDAY EVENING, 19 MARCH 1879
ROOM THREE, THREE CRIPPLES PUBLIC HOUSE
EASTON, BRISTOL, ENGLAND

It was a well-used, seldom cleaned room, poorly lit by a single candle on the lopsided table near the wretched, ragged bed. Over the bed was a colored print, in an ill-formed and badly chipped frame, representing a naval engagement. A couple men-of-war were banging away at each other most vigorously as another vessel burned in the background. In the foreground were broken masts and blue legs sticking out of the water.

Beneath the pictorial carnage was the very real body of the disreputable character known as Bad Bill, at least to those who only knew of him, or those who knew him just barely. Among those who had experienced the misfortune of actually interacting with him, he was more frequently known as That Bastard Bill. No one seemed to know his last name, or to care, but various people had various thoughts regarding the source of his intermittent, occasionally substantial income.

Detective John Reeves leaned over the body, paying particular attention to the entry wound in the center of the forehead. Just five days earlier, Reeves had examined a somewhat similar entry wound, the one in the center of Lt. William Perenna's forehead. While the two wounds were similar in some regards, including the nearly perfect placement in the center of the forehead, the most recent wound was not as torn and ragged as had been the earlier one. Still, Bill's wound was not as quite as circular as John Reeves had come to expect. More curiously, Bill's wound was surrounded by a ring, an annulus, of tiny black dots and a broader band of fine soot. Also, Bill did not have any mysterious residue on his left hand, on either hand.

Detective Reeves, therefore, was tempted to cast off any similarity as mere coincidence, and he would have done so had it not been for the boots so neatly placed by the door.

"Take him to Central Station," said Reeves to the constables standing behind him. "I want Dr. Weston to perform the autopsy."

The two constables heaved Bill from the bed and dropped him, with a fleshy thump, onto the police stretcher they had spread open on the floor.

"The boots," said Reeves, pointing toward the pair near the door. "Take them with him."

The constable nearer the door grabbed both boots with one hand and unceremoniously plopped them on Bill's chest. There, they somehow found sufficient purchase not to slide off.

Rigor had only just begun to set in, so, while Bill's fingers and toes had become nearly rigid, his arms and legs swung free, banging against the stairway balusters as the constables carried his stretcher down. In the parlor, the few patrons who still remained for questioning stepped toward the grisly procession to get one last look at their friend, colleague, or nemesis. Each one's attention was carried first to the hole in the man's forehead.

Remaining upstairs, Reeves examined the room, paying particular attention to the wall behind the bed, hunting for a bullet hole. He found none. The large amount of blood spattered on the bed and wall evidenced an exit wound, and the bullet had to be somewhere. He tossed the filthy bedding, shaking it to free any entangled bullet fragment, freeing only dirt, dust, and dried bits of food. He examined the thin, disgusting mattress, but found nothing of interest, certainly nothing as significant as a bullet that had just taken a man's life. He moved the bed frame from the wall and examined the region beneath. There was a profusion of rat droppings, but no bullet fragment kept them company.

He examined the wall again, but still found no bullet hole. He pulled the bottom of the naval battle print slightly from the wall, peeked behind, and smiled. There it was. He let the print settle back against the wall, keeping a mental note of where the hole would be in the painting, nodding his head slowly when finally seeing it. What looked superficially to be a gigantic cannonball hole in the side of one ship was in fact a tiny bullet hole in a cheap print of a regrettable painting. Reeves removed the print from the wall and set it beside the door, deciding it was evidence, deciding also that it would be a nice trophy for his office.

He examined the bullet hole, pulled his clasp knife from his pocket, and pried the bullet fragment from the wall. The fragment was flattened, just as flat as had been the fragment dug from the wall of the Perenna home. The current fragment looked a bit larger than the Perenna fragment. He would weigh it once he returned to Central Station. The Perenna fragment weighed fifty-six grains; this one would weigh somewhat more. If it weighed more than eighty, it could not possibly have come from a thirty-six-caliber roundball. Perhaps a thirty-six conical, or a forty-four.

Perhaps, thought Reeves, he would have Weston dig through Bill's inert brain in search of any fragment remaining within. In retrospect, he should have had Weston recover any fragments from within Perenna's skull. Too late for that now. No matter, though. Determining the weight of That Bastard

Bill's fragment would still be informative. Reeves dropped the fragment in his pocket, took a final glance around the room, and departed.

In the parlor, his junior detective, Sergeant Witcham Fendall, was nearly finished questioning the last of the guests and patrons. Younger, shorter and thicker set than Reeves, and marked by the pox, Fendall usually carried something of a reserved and thoughtful air, as if he were engaged in deep philosophical thought. He had, nonetheless, a diligent bent in pursuing private inquiries of a delicate nature, and thus was well suited for interviewing reluctant guests and patrons.

Reeves handed Fendall the confiscated painting and walked to the bar. There, Reeves summoned the proprietor, using his demeanor rather than his words. Flashing his badge to confirm the obvious, he asked, "Name?"

"Stagg."

"Tell me about the shooter."

"I already talked to him," replied Stagg, pointing to Reeves's junior.

"He's forgetful. Tell me."

"Not much to tell. He came in, sat at that table close to the door, and bought nothing. Just sat there, looking about. Bill gets up, goes upstairs, the fella follows him. We hear a gunshot, and the fella walks back down here, as calm as you want. Walks over here, 'bout where you're standin', takes a bit of a drink, walks out the door. Like I say, not much to tell."

"You know the man?"

"Never saw him before."

"Sergeant!" Reeves shouted over his shoulder, without taking his eyes off Stagg. "Anyone see the shooter before?"

"No, sir. No one."

"Describe him," ordered Reeves, returning his attention to the proprietor.

"Not much to describe, either."

"Try."

"I don't know. Normal height and weight I guess. Thin moustache, in need of a shave, but no beard or side-whiskers, Neither the poorest or the richest of 'em, at least from his clothes. Long coat, and a hat, pretty much like everybody in here. Large hat, though, not a cap. Kept it pulled down pretty far. Never took it off, 'cept once. I noticed that about him."

"Tell me about the once."

"Came downstairs, calm like I said, at least he seemed so. But when he comes over here, before he takes his drink, he takes off his hat and wipes his forehead."

"Because he was sweating," asked Reeves.

"Yeah, but that's not the only thing I noticed about him. I remember it now."

"Remember it aloud."

"His head was dented in, right here." Stagg put a finger to a spot just above his right temple. "Part covered by his hair, but not all covered. Guess that's why he kept his hat on. Didn't want people staring at his dented head."

"Who would?"

"Not me."

"Thank you, Mr. Stagg."

"Who's going to pay for the picture ya took?"

"Send the bill to Disraeli. Mention me by name."

chapter nine
FAILURE TO COMPEL

Wednesday morning, 19 March 1879
Bristol Police Central Station, Bridewell Street
Bristol, England

After making their way through streets deeply mudded by the most recent rain, the cab carrying Louise and Lindsey moored alongside the Central Station. Going ashore by way of a gangplank laid over the mud, they entered the newly white-washed lobby, to encounter a desk sergeant working with a pen, ink, and ruler, posting up his books as studiously as if he were a monk in a monastery atop a mountain. From the cells beyond came the howling fury of a drunken woman banging herself against the bars.

"Detective Reeves, please," said Lindsey over the clamor.

The sergeant stopped writing long enough point his pen down a hallway.

With Lindsey in the lead, the two made their way down the hallway, almost immediately obstructed by a melancholy lad in white-splotched clothing, with a bucket of whitewash at his feet and a long-handled brush in his hand. The young man glanced at the two visitors, and then, to make room, backed a bit down the long stretch of hallway still unpainted. Life to him seemed hollow; his existence but a burden. He stepped aside for their passage only reluctantly. Sighing deeply, he returned to his task, dipped his brush and swabbed it listlessly along the wall.

"I'll show you my sore toe," said Louise, turning suddenly, "if you'll let me paint a bit."

He stopped and stared. He looked at her bandaged foot, then looked back up at her smiling round face, his confusion as obvious as a tarantula on a teacake.

"You don't gotta show me your toe. You can paint the entire building for free."

Louise laughed kindly, to the extent that is possible, and patted the miserable painter on his cheek.

"*Adventures of Tom Sawyer* by Mark Twain," she said in explanation. "Give it a read. I assure you, life won't seem so dreary."

His bewilderment abated not at all. As she turned to continue her hobble down the hall, Lindsey shook his head in wonderment. She shooed him along with a smile and a flick of her fingers.

John Reeves's office was the last one on the left. Lindsey tapped with his knuckles on the open door and walked in. Louise followed. As she entered, Reeves's visage transformed from mild aggravation to pleasant surprise.

"Good to see you again, Miss Hawkins," he said, rising from his chair with a smile, walking around his desk. "And you, sir. I don't believe we've met."

"David Lindsey, *Bristol North Star*," he said, shaking Reeves's outstretched hand.

"Of course. This must be about the Perenna case. Have a seat," Reeves said to Louise.

Lindsey and Louise settled into simple wooden chairs, sturdy but in serious need of refinishing. Reeves regained his own chair on the opposite side of the cluttered desk. He closed the folder immediately in front of him and slipped it into the desk's top right drawer.

"How might I assist you?" he asked.

"We understand you have another murder on your hands," offered Lindsey, as an opener.

"I have many on my hands, sir."

"More specifically, then, another body with a bullet hole in the center of the forehead."

"How is it that you come to know of this?"

"I'm a reporter."

"Of course," Reeves muttered.

"So?"

"Yes, we do indeed have such a body in the dead room."

"May we see it?"

Reeves looked at Louise, who betrayed no emotion, then looked back at Lindsey.

"Not at this time, though I appreciate your seeking permission, unlike last Sunday morning."

Heat shot through Louise, from scalp to the pit of her stomach. The guilty feeling of having been caught flushed her cheeks. Then she realized that John Reeves thought no less of her for having participated in the invasion of his dead room. She detected his incipient smile, noticeable not at all to Lindsey, and she regained her equanimity.

"The next time you find yourself there," Reeves continued, "you might consider checking the shadows."

Lindsey was irrepressible.

"Banished forever, am I?"

"For now, at least."

"Then my employee, Jeffers? May he examine the body? Or Miss Hawkins, for that matter?"

Reeves shook his head slowly from side to side.

"Same reason?"

Reeves nodded.

"Even if an innocent woman's life depends on it?"

"What makes you think she's innocent?"

Louise almost broke her silence, but caught herself. *Not yet*, she thought.

"The same person seems to have shot both victims, yet Mrs. Perenna was, still is, behind bars when the second man was shot at the Three Cripples."

The conversation seized as each appraised the other.

"You must have something more than that," Reeves finally said, "else you would not have bothered coming here."

"Both wounds were in the center of the forehead, *and* both were ragged rather than circular."

"Not quite, Sir. The first wound was torn in a stellate pattern. The perimeter of the second was indeed ragged rather than neatly circular, but the skin certainly wasn't ripped, as in the case of Lt. Perenna."

Reeves leaned back in his chair and folded his arms over his chest, making himself comfortable as he waited for Lindsey to show his hand. The location and shape of the entry wound were easy. He could have talked to any number of people at the Three Cripples. Anything else of substance would be considerably harder to discover.

"Alright," said Louise, slowly. "Both wounds were in the center of the forehead, *and —*" she paused for effect, "*—* the bullets were recovered from the wall and weighed nearly the same."

Reeves unfolded his arms and sat upright, trying belatedly to control his reaction. *Drat!* he thought. *That would be it for Fendell, or whoever the hell it was that slipped the information to the press.*

"No one told us, Detective Reeves," she said, quietly, "other than you, just now. I simply guessed. And guessed correctly, obviously."

Reeves closed his eyes, leaned back again, and crossed his arms again. She had read him before like a book, and now she had read him again.

"Off the record?" Reeves asked, without opening his eyes.

"Yes," answered Lindsey, "but not if necessary to save the life of an innocent."

"It will be of no use for that purpose," said Reeves, returning to a more attentive posture, glancing from Lindsey to Louise. "The information could, however, if carelessly reported, result in an unjustified panic, such as the Ripper frenzy in London last year. That might sell papers, Mr. Lindsey, but the police certainly don't want something like that here."

"I understand," said Lindsey.

"So I have your word that this discussion will be off the record?"

"If I have your word that the information cannot save Mrs. Perenna."

"You have my word."

"Then you have mine."

Reeves heaved a sigh before beginning.

"The bullet fragment we extracted from the Perenna wall weighed fifty-six grains. It was a fragment, not the entire bullet. In retrospect, I should have had Dr. Weston extract the other fragments from Lt. Perenna's brain during the autopsy."

He paused to gauge Louise's reaction to such blunt discussion.

"The bullet fragment I plucked from the wall of Room Three at the Three Cripples weighed sixty-one grains. It was also a fragment, flattened in much the same fashion as was the Perenna fragment."

Lindsey scribbled notes furiously.

"This time I asked Dr. Weston to extract all the fragments he could find still in the victim's brain. He informed me, he showed me actually, that there were three more fragments large enough to extract and weigh, and a plethora of tiny fragments too small and too numerous to deal with. The total weight of the four largest fragments was seventy-four grains. I'm guessing the total weight of the bullet in each case was eighty grains, the weight of a thirty-six-caliber roundball. I don't know of any other bullet close to that weight."

"So both victims were shot in the center of the forehead," asked Lindsey, "with a thirty-six-caliber revolver?"

"Both with a thirty-six-caliber *handgun*. Certainly a revolver in the case of William Perenna, possibly, probably a revolver in the case of the Three Cripples victim."

"Bastard Bill?" asked Lindsey.

"We don't know the victim's full name," replied Reeves. "We may not even know his first name, for that matter."

"Explain to me then, how the similar weight of the bullets, and the same caliber of murder weapon, would not help save Mrs. Perenna."

"The bullet weight and the handgun caliber might be the same, but the shooter certainly is not."

"How can you be so sure that the locations of the wounds, their non-circular aspects, the bullet weights, *and* the weapon calibers are simply coincidence?"

"Coincidences happen all the time, Mr. Lindsey. That's why we have a word for them. The point here is that the shooter is a different person, though the wounds, bullets, and weapons are similar. The shooter at the Three Cripples made no effort to rush out without being noticed. He simply walked from the room, without even shutting the door behind himself, much less locking the door in some mysterious fashion as if from the inside. He calmly walked down the steps, went to the bar, sipped a drink, pocketed a cake, and walked out the front door."

The room fell silent as each pondered the possibilities.

"Does that sound like the Perenna shooter to you, Miss Hawkins?" asked Reeves quietly.

She replied after a moment's reflection. "No, it does not."

The three of them sat in quiet, Lindsey waiting for Louise to discuss the trigonometry, Reeves wishing that he might sometime engage her in less distressing circumstance, and she adding up the facts.

"He's killed before," said Louise, to Reeves's utter amazement. "This shooter at the Three Cripples, you know that he's killed before. You've been hunting for him."

A heavy hush fell over the room. Even the woman screaming from the cells stopped at that very moment, almost as if she could hear the conversation in the little office at the end of a narrow hallway, far from the bars against which she had recently been banging her head.

Lindsey, sensing Reeves's reaction, realized that he had stumbled upon another story, perhaps an even bigger story.

"A multiple murderer?" asked Lindsey, his excitement barely contained.

"I remind you, Mr. Lindsey, that everything you learn in this room is off the record."

"When I gave that promise, we were speaking only of the shooting at the Three Cripples."

"We were speaking of the shooter," clarified Reeves, his agitation becoming apparent. "If your promises are so narrow and malleable, then we have nothing more to speak of."

Lindsey suddenly felt like a tightly leashed bloodhound on a hot scent. *Damn!* he swore to himself. *Damn!*

"You are correct," he managed to say out loud, "and I will stand by my word."

"I would expect nothing less of you, Mr. Lindsey, else I would not reveal even as much as I have."

"So you are confirming your pursuit of a multiple murderer?"

"I am not. Nor will I speak any more of the shooter at the Three Cripples, having already satisfied you that he is not the one who shot Lt. Perenna."

"You realize, Detective Reeves," interjected Louise, "that the Three Cripples shooter was aware of the details of the shooting at Torquay Terrace."

"Of course," Reeves replied, to Lindsey's growing frustration.

"And he has done this before," she continued calmly, "this mimicking murderer."

Reeves did not reply. Lindsey mindlessly flipped his pencil in the air, allowing it to fall to the ground. He hung his head, chin to his chest, eyes closed firmly. *Mimicking Murderer!* He could see the banner headline that would not be published by his paper.

"How many times has he killed?" asked Louise, calmly.

Reeves gave no response, none verbally at least, or any by change of expression, he hoped.

"Five?" asked Louise, reading him, making him uncomfortable. "Ten?"

"No more of this, Miss Hawkins," said Reeves suddenly and firmly. "If you have no more questions regarding the Perenna shooting, then I'll bid you farewell. I have work to do."

"Even if the two murders were by different shooters," Louise replied, without a beat, "Anna Perenna is not one of them. She is innocent. I calculate it to be so."

Reeves barely avoided the temptation to smile, hoping beyond hope, he feared, that she would not again see through his mask. "Please explain."

"I gained entrance to the Perenna House —"

"*We* gained entrance," interrupted Lindsey, unwilling to allow Louise to accept full responsibility for the illegal act.

"*We* gained entrance and made careful measurements of all pertinent distances and heights. There can be no doubt that if Anna Perenna shot her husband in the forehead, then the bullet would have traveled from the revolver to the forehead at an eight-degree angle above the horizontal. But the bullet path through Lt. Perenna's skull was nearly horizontal. My most likely conclusion is that someone substantially taller than Anna Perenna fired the shot."

Reeves was not surprised, after observing their foray into the dead room, that the two of them had broken into the Perenna house. He had no more desire to charge them for that trespass than for the one into his dead room.

"I should have made those measurements myself," he admitted.

She nodded in agreement.

"You mentioned your *most likely* conclusion, so you have some doubt?"

"There is little doubt."

"But you have some, no matter how small?"

She pursed her lips, unhappy to concede the point. He suddenly had her on the defensive, and she did not care for it.

"What is it that gives you pause?" he pressed.

"My calculation presumes that the lieutenant was holding his head erect in normal fashion when he was shot."

"But you are aware of at least one other explanation for the bullet traveling directly from the front to the back of his head?"

"He may have been looking down at an eight-degree angle, the same angle at which the bullet traveled upward."

"In which case he would have been looking directly at the weapon that killed him?

"Yes."

"But you don't believe that's what happened?"

"No."

"Why is that?"

"Because he was standing twelve inches from the wall. If the bullet had been travelling upwards at an eight degree angle, then the bullet hole in the wall would be approximately two inches higher than it is."

"Twelve inches multiplied by the sine of eight inches," replied Reeves, "is less than two inches."

She looked at him, impressed somewhat that he understood the trigonometry, somewhat more that he properly incorporated the units, and even more that he so quickly and easily challenged her approximation.

"One and two thirds inches, actually."

"Quite close to that," Reeves replied with a smirk. After a moment, he went on. "Assume that Lt. Perenna was standing directly against the wall. Then, even if his head had been inclined at an eight-degree angle, gazing down at the barrel of the revolver his wife was pointing at him, the bullet would not have had the time and distance to climb an inch and two thirds before impacting the wall. It would have entered the wall just at the same height as the exit wound, exactly where you found it."

"You would be correct, Detective, if he had indeed been standing against the wall. I can assure you, however, that he was standing twelve inches from the wall, as I have already explained."

"And how are you so sure of that, Miss Hawkins?"

She hesitated, inexplicably shy about prostrating herself on the floor of the Perennas' front room, in search of wool fragments. Why should that bother her now? Worse, she could see in Reeves's face that he sensed her discomfort, which, to her surprise, somehow added to her unease.

Sitting slightly straighter, she said, "I examined the floor carefully, with a magnifying lens. As his stocking feet slipped from beneath him, wool fibers from the lieutenant's stockings, small and difficult to detect, snagged on the rough boards."

"And you could read those fibers."

"As easily as I can read A. M. Barnard. The fibers began twelve inches from the wall."

"So those fibers are the basis of your argument that Mrs. Perenna must be innocent."

"Yes," conceded Louise, concealing a sudden anxiety.

"And because you found no fibers within twelve inches of the wall, and because of your trigonometric calculations based thereon, you expect that a dozen jurymen, none of them likely to be skilled in mathematics, each more than likely distrustful of a woman's intellect, will declare Anna Perenna to be not guilty?"

A pall fell over the room. A pall. At least that is the word that came to Louise's mind as her confidence slipped away.

Her thoughts flashed to Stoddart's *Reminiscences of Dickens*: "When the pall of night is enshrouding us in Chimerian darkness, when we are ready to stand on the brink of the great mystery, shall our thoughts be of fleshy vanities?"

The detective's question had caused her to envision herself in the witness box, scoffed at by the jurymen and the barristers and the crowd. She heard the whispering of loss. She felt the tug of peaceful resignation, the soothing warmth of acquiescence, each encouraging her to quit, to give it up, to bow out, to allow the justice system to run its course without her.

"I could not help you, Miss Hawkins," said Reeves quietly, "even if I believed Anna Perenna to be innocent, which I do not. It is beyond my powers to intervene in what is now a matter for courts and lawyers."

"I thank you for your time, then," she said, rising and making her way from the room, Lindsey at her heels.

Reeves slumped back in his chair, pursed his lips, and squeezed shut his eyes. Each time he met her, he felt more thoroughly how truly lonely he was.

WEDNESDAY AFTERNOON, 19 MARCH 1879
THE GUILDHALL, BROAD STREET
BRISTOL, ENGLAND

Though he would not see them in his dilapidated office, Anna Perenna's solicitor, Andrew Mallard, agreed to escort them to the office of Anna Perenna's barrister, one Mr. Charles Stinson, Esquire.

Although appearing to be a teenaged lad, Mallard was full-grown. He had a nervous manner and a painful hesitation in his speech. It did not appear to be a natural defect, but seemed rather the result of timidity, arising from the consciousness of being kept down by want of means, or interest, or connection, or physical stature, as the case might be.

Stinson's lobby was an uncarpeted room of tolerable dimensions, with a large writing table drawn up near the fire, the baize top of which had long since lost all claim to its original hue of green, gradually grown gray with dust and age, except where all traces of natural color were obliterated by ink stains. Upon the table were numerous bundles of papers tied with strips of red cloth. Behind it sat an elderly clerk whose sleek appearance and heavy gold watch chain presented imposing indications of the extensive and lucrative practice of the barrister Stinson.

After warning the visitors that Mr. Stinson was exceptionally busy, the clerk disappeared into the legal luminary's sanctum, whence he shortly returned on tiptoe, and informed the visitors that Mr. Stinson had been prevailed upon, in violation of all established rules and customs, to admit them at once.

The barrister was still writing when his guests were shown in.

"Ah!" he said, putting his pen carefully in the inkstand, rising, walking around to greet his guests, nursing his left leg in the process.

Stinson was a lantern-faced, sallow-complexioned man, of about five and forty. He had those dull-looking, boiled eyes that are often to be seen in the heads of people who have applied themselves during many years to a weary and laborious course of study. His squint would have been sufficient, without the additional eyeglass that dangled from a broad black ribbon at his neck, to warn a stranger that he was nearsighted.

His hair was thin and weak, partly attributable to his having never devoted much time to its arrangement, and partly to his having worn for twenty-five years the forensic wig that hung on a block beside his desk. The marks of hair powder on his coat collar, and the ill-washed and badly tied white neckerchief around his throat, showed that he had not found sufficient leisure since he left the court to make any alteration in his dress. The slovenly style of the remainder of his costume warranted the inference that his personal appearance would not have been very much improved if he had.

Books of practice, heaps of papers, and opened letters were scattered over his desk, without any attempt at order or arrangement. The furniture was old and rickety. Four frail guest chairs were scattered about the room. The doors of the bookcase were rotting about their hinges. Dust flew out from the carpet in little clouds at every step. The blinds were yellow with age and dirt. The state of everything in the room showed, with a clearness not to be mistaken, that Mr. Charles Stinson was far too occupied with his professional pursuits to pay any great heed or regard to his personal comforts.

"We have not had the pleasure of meeting face to face," he said to Mallard, easily recognizing him as the solicitor among the trio, "but I have been through all your paperwork, just now. Well prepared, I must say. Thorough."

"Most generous of you, sir," replied Mallard. "Most kind, indeed. This is a trivial case of course, not in its effect, to be sure, but certainly in its demands for preparation. And of course I am well aware of your work, Mr. Stinson. Always brilliant, sir, I assure you."

"Uhm, right, right," said Stinson, in no need of Mallard's toadying. "And you must be the reporter," Stinson said, turning to shake Lindsey's hand.

"David Lindsey, *Bristol North Star*."

"And you," Stinson said, taking Louise's fingertips in his hand and bowing, "must be the interested party."

"Louise Hawkins," she replied, with the slightest nod and curtsy.

"Please be seated," Stinson said, offering one of his questionable guest chairs to Louise, allowing the others to fend for themselves. He then stepped back around his desk and took his own armchair, which moaned and creaked as he settled in.

"I forewarn you that this must be brief, Miss Hawkins," cautioned Stinson. "I have more cases on my plate that I might hope to manage, and in most others, I have some hope of compensation. We should therefore get straight to the point. I understand that you claim to have evidence of Mrs. Perenna's innocence, none of which, I might add, do I see in Mr. Mallard's paperwork."

Mallard prepared to launch into a simpering defense of his paperwork but was stifled by a single upraised finger from the barrister.

"I want to hear directly from Miss Hawkins," said Stinson, estimating her potentiality as a witness.

"Do you have any sense of trigonometry, sir?" asked Louise.

"Long forgotten," Stinson replied. "I hope that it is not important to the presentation of your evidence of innocence."

"May I draw you a picture, sir?"

"Only a verbal one, since that is all that you would be allowed to present before a jury."

"A demonstration then?"

"One that I might recreate before a jury?"

"Yes, if you are clever."

Recognizing Louise as the clever one, Stinson said only, "Proceed."

"Mr. Lindsey, help me, if you will. Please stand one foot from that wall."

"Why one foot from the wall?" interrupted Stinson.

Louise took a deep breath. "I will explain in a moment."

"Now, Miss Hawkins. Not later. Now, if you please, since it seems to trouble you. And it now troubles me, and I have yet to know what it is. Why do you ask Mr. Lindsey to stand one foot from the wall rather than, more naturally, against the wall, or near the wall. Why precisely one foot?"

"Because that is how far Lt. Perenna was standing from the wall when he was shot."

Stinson thumbed through the papers before him.

"I don't see that anywhere in Mr. Mallard's documentation."

Mallard began to speak but was silenced by an index finger.

"I deduced it," declared Louise.

Stinson laughed, not long or hard, but enough to cut. Mallard joined Stinson in his merriment, careful to laugh neither louder nor longer than did his superior.

"Hear her out," Lindsey insisted, not without force.

"Very well," said Stinson. "How did you deduce that Lt. Perenna was standing one foot from the wall when he was shot?"

Louise told him about the sock fibers on the wool floorboards.

"How do you know this?"

"I witnessed the scene almost immediately after the shooting."

"Yes, I do see that in the paperwork."

"He was nearly supine, except that his head still leaned against the base of the wall. In considering both the position in which he lay, and the bloody streak where his head slid down the wall, I deduced that his stocking feet slid from beneath him as he sank."

"You deduced all that from glancing at the body for just a moment."

"Yes," replied Louise, as Stinson nodded and smiled, as Mallard chuckled.

"Do you find this difficult, Miss Hawkins, submitting to such impolite questioning, to such mockery?"

She stood her ground, but did not answer.

"Of course you do, Miss Hawkins. Who would not? Be aware that this is but a taste of what you would receive in a court of law were you to relate such evidence of innocence in support of a woman who has already effectively confessed to the murder for which she is charged."

"After the inquest," Louise pressed on, determined to hold nothing back, "I re-entered the Perenna residence by scaling the back wall and picking the lock to the back door."

Stinson *tried* to suppress a laugh, one brought on by the thought of such a short woman, hampered by her voluminous clothing, attempting to scale a wall—tried, and failed. Mallard also. Stinson wheeled his chair around to hide, or to highlight, his laughter. Mallard doubled over. Neither had, in his career, been so entertained.

Lindsey could take no more. "That's not the only evidence we have!" he nearly shouted, rising and slamming an open palm atop Simpson's desk. "There is the entry wound, also. We'll soon be shooting bullets into pigs' heads to better understand *that*."

From the lobby, the old clerk heard queer sounds coming from the inner office, sounds that had never before passed through Mr. Stinson's closed door—those of riotous laughter.

chapter ten

MR. JACOB DIX

"There's no Colt Navy revolver to be found," Louise flatly declared, dropping into one of Lindsey's Trafalgar chairs, laying aside her single crutch, and counting on her fingers. "I've been to every ironmonger in or near Bristol: Albert's, Cartwright and Son, Croft's, Cowlishaw's, Gardiner and Sons, Hulbert and Company, Meatyard's, Motley's, and Tonk's. I've been offered Adams Mark I, Mark II, and Mark III revolvers, a Beaumont-Adams, a Colt .31 caliber, multiple Colt .44 calibers, any number of Enfields, an ancient Howdah, a not-quite-so-old Lancaster, and even a five-barrel Nordenfelt rapid-fire. Mostly, I've been told that a lady such as myself would be better served by some sort of pepperbox, the least subtle of which was the Mariette, with its twenty-four barrels. Where I might carry such a weapon, I have no idea."

"Do you always alphabetize your lists?" asked Lindsey.

"Only when I am out of sorts. And other than Jeremy, you're the first to notice. The mongers all tell the same story: Colt Navy revolvers are in astonishingly short supply, at least in England, because British military officers are required to provide their own service revolver, and they frequently insist on having this exact model, due to its reliability and durability. Not only do the mongers not have a single Colt Navy among their wares, each has a list of officers awaiting one, and would sooner sell to a member of Her Majesty's army than do business with a lady who would, in any event, be better served by a floral-engraved six-shot Worcester."

"Perhaps we could settle for a Remington," said Lindsey, crossing his arms in thought. "It's similar."

"And anything we might learn would be dismissed, because William Perenna was killed with a Colt Navy. Might the police allow you to borrow the Colt they recovered from the Perenna house?"

"Perhaps instead they can be convinced to just release her, then we wouldn't need to trouble with testing at all," Lindsey responded sarcastically.

"Unlikely then?"

"Less likely than you finding a Colt Navy. I have a thought: since military officers are the ones with the Colts, we might get hold of a military officer and persuade him to let us use his."

"But they seem to cherish them so. Do you know any who might lend us one?"

"No. I am aware, however, that officers arrive from abroad by the score in Bristol, most of them longing for wine, women, and song. One desiring pocket cash might have put his revolver in hock anticipating his next disbursement, and somehow never reclaimed the gun. Perhaps we can find a pawn shop with a Colt Navy for sale."

"That, sir," said Louise, visibly encouraged, "is a good thought."

THURSDAY AFTERNOON, 20 MARCH 1879
BROAD QUAY
BRISTOL, ENGLAND

There were forty-nine pawnbrokers in Bristol. Using a combination of cab, tram, feet, and crutches, Louise and Lindsey visited Stanley Alfred, the Alman Brothers, Robinson Charles, William Freenan, Spink and Son, Arthur Theobald, and Henry Watts, not in that order, and with no success. Forgoing the midday meal, they forged on. There were still many other shops to visit if they had no success with the next one, the one on Broad Quay.

Though by no means in formal attire, they stood out among the longshoremen, the laborers and the rabble of the docks who manned the ships, worked the quay, picked the pockets, peddled the wares, peddled themselves, and sat, caps in hand, against the decaying pillars of each dock. The din was remarkable, but more intrusive was the smell, which was, by itself, almost another member of the multitude. Low tide, hot tar, rotting fish, and unwashed humanity combined in a sense-numbing stench. One odiferous beggar with a horrendously twisted lip looked so desperately needful that Louise dropped a coin into his cap.

"Ga' bleff ya," he slurred. "Piddy 'bout ya fut."

Louise nodded and gave him a gentle smile.

"Half of them are professional beggars," said Lindsey, drawing her away. "A few of them may be better off than you."

"So I have heard," said Louise.

"Does that not bother you?"

"It certainly affects the mathematics of the situation. If you are correct about half of them not being in need of the money, then I still have a fifty-percent chance of helping someone who is in need. Alternatively, I can perceive of my contribution as having a fifty-percent return on my charity. I am satisfied with that investment."

"Even if he truly needs the money, he is likely to invest it in drink," Lindsey said.

"Perhaps that is what he most needs at the moment."

"You surprise me yet again, Miss Hawkins."

Louise said nothing in reply, focusing instead on the horse-drawn wooden sleds transporting goods to and from the ships docked nearby. Even the wheel, she thought, had yet to find its way to this forsaken place.

"When we were speaking with Detective Reeves," said Lindsey after a bit, "you again mentioned A. M. Barnard. Tell me more of her."

"She had a tendency," explained Louise, launching into one of her dithyrambs, "to publish her more sensational writings under her pseudonym. She explained that, what she called her blood and thunder works, are easier to compose and considerably more lucrative than the moral and elaborate works of Shakespeare. In *The Mummy's Curse*, for example, she wrote of a mummified sorceress discovered in the pyramid of Cheops. Against dire warnings on a piece of parchment, the archaeologist burned the mummified body but preserved the coffin. He thereafter suffered one misfortune after another, each seeming to relate somehow back to his burning of the mummified sorceress. It is another of Barnard's archetypal enchantress tales, a theme she returns to frequently.

"Her family were staunch abolitionists, their home once a station along the Underground Railroad. She came to know John Brown, William Lloyd Garrison, and even Frederick Douglass. In the War Between the States, she worked as a nurse at a Union hospital until struck down with typhoid. The thought of her efforts to free slaves makes me ponder, in unfavorable fashion, the sordid slavery history of this aging port town. Bristol grew rich off the enslavement of the sable sons and daughters of Africa, not by enslaving them directly, instead by building and outfitting ships that would transport them from Africa to America, under the most horrific conditions imaginable. More than two thousand ships left from here to Africa, from there to transport more than a half million Africans to America. Did you know that, Mr. Lindsey?"

"Not in the detail you now provide, no."

"Do you feel that now, the weight of all those chains, the sting of all those whips?"

"There is no way that I can feel the full weight, but it is certainly distressing and depressing to think of it. At least slave ships are now an abomination of our past."

"And now this port," observed Louise, "once the second most prosperous in the country, struggles for its share of shipping."

"Perhaps it would be more vibrant now had they not built it eight miles from the Channel," said Lindsey, meandering off on his own jeremiad. "It is connected only by this meager, winding Avon, which twice each day is little more than mud. Yet they hope to solve the problem by straightening it some more, or filling it with more dams and locks. Even as we speak, there are more proposals and promises going before the council. I have repeatedly editorialized against throwing good money after bad."

Lindsey dropped twopence into a beggar's cap. Louise smiled at the cleverness of his investment. The old man said, "Thank ya, guv."

"I am of two minds about the improvement of these docks," said Louise. "Part of me hopes they will thrive and bring prosperity to many. Another part of me hopes they will fail and disappear forever, as punishment for the misery they helped inflict. Of course, children should not suffer for the crimes of their parents, but still—"

Louise's voice trailed off as she struggled not to fall into a blue funk.

They arrived at their next destination in short order, as indicated by the weather-beaten shingle above the door: *Jacob Dix, Pawnbroker.* Outside stood a tiny flower girl peddling clusters of cowslips, probably plucked from fields nearby. Louise handed a shilling to the child, picked a single stem of fragrant yellow bells from the sparse inventory, and said to the child, "This is for me, and that's for you." She gave the little girl a smile, as kind and sweet as Lindsey had ever witnessed. The waif stared momentarily at her newfound fortune before, without a word or gesture in return, running off.

Dix's pawnshop was much like the others. Through windows begrimed with the airborne filth of years, Louise and Lindsey could see a jumble of articles intended to lure in innocent passersby: silver teapots, well-worn saucepans, gold watches, rusty flatirons, a carpenter's chisel, and unlikeliest of all, an ivory-framed mirror hand painted on the back with the portrait of a fashionable beauty. Louise noted the ironic arrangement of incongruous items, the useful and useless placed in juxtaposition, trifles mingled with necessities. A porcelain Dresden figure, brightly hued and dainty, for example, stood next to a copper warming pan.

Beyond the door, the goods were no better arranged. A silver-handled dagger of the Renaissance lay with a score of cheap dinner knives. An ape's taxidermied paw touched an agate saucer holding patinated coins of all ages and nations. Watches, in alternate rows of gold and silver, dangled on their chains over temples of ivory minutely carved by Chinese artificers. On a square of rich silk brocade, multicolored as a parrot's plumage, were piled a careless profusion of medals, charms, old-fashioned rings set with dim gems, and the frail glass bangles of Indian dancing girls.

Louise took everything in. Talismans of coral from Southern Italy, designed to avert the evil eye. A small black cabinet of Japanese lacquer adorned with gilded grotesques. Jeweled pipes of Turkey, set roughly with blue turquoise stones like tiny scraps of summer sky. Georgian caps with embroideries of tarnished gold. Amulets, earrings, bracelets, snuffboxes, and mosaic brooches from Florence, overlaid with fine gray dust, representing the flotsam of many centuries, the dry bones of a hundred social systems dead or dying.

"You'll only encourage her," growled the pawnbroker. "The little brat will be back tomorrow, and so will a dozen like her, blocking my door and harassing my customers."

From the other brokers they had already visited, Louise and Lindsey understood, even before they entered his shop, that Jacob Dix was so old that no one knew his real age, that he was so grotesque as to be jeered at by children in the streets, and that his avarice had earned him the name Skinflint among his colleagues, themselves hardly generous. If Jacob Dix possessed a single good quality to counterbalance his many bad ones, no person they'd met had described it. Perhaps those men had not troubled to look. Surly and uncommunicative, no one reported going near him, save to transact business, to wrangle endlessly with him during the transaction, and to curse him at its conclusion. Now that Louise and Lindsey found themselves actually before him, as he stood behind the narrow counter that spanned his shop, his voice and words and visage reinforced all they had been told.

The counter was divided into four sentry boxes by wooden screens. Two of the boxes were occupied by customers desperate for cash. Racked by a constant cough, Dix wrangled with both suppliants nearly simultaneously, using skills honed over decades, as if he were a grandmaster playing multiple games of chess against multiple opponents. He was rumored to fight over every farthing and to begrudge every payment, as if every coin was a drop of blood wrung from his withered heart.

Lindsey stepped into the rightmost sentry box and Louise hobbled up behind, flower stem still in hand. After dismissing a man who insisted on a half penny more than Dix was willing to pay, the proprietor appeared in front of them, and glared.

"We're looking for a Colt Navy revolver," said Lindsey.

"Ain't got one," sniffed the pawnbroker.

"We're willing to pay good money," said Lindsey.

"Very hard to find," Dix said. "Very expensive."

"But you might be able to find one?"

"For a price."

"We're willing to pay three pounds."

Dix moved away, bringing up some wet-sounding phlegm and hawking it into a brass spittoon set on the floor behind him.

"Four pounds," Lindsey called after him.

Dix did not reappear, though his coughing placed him nearby.

"Five," said Lindsey, leaning over the counter to be heard, but the ancient miser had re-engaged his only other remaining customer, an increasingly desperate longshoreman at the far box.

"Mr. Dix," tried Louise, "we wish to rent the Colt Navy revolver that you have in your possession, for one month, at a non-compounded annual rate of two thousand four hundred percent of the weapon's value."

"Five p, that's my final offer," Dix told his other customer.

"The missus'll kill me if I return with only five," the customer beseeched. "It belonged to her mother, you see, and her mother beyond that."

Dix's silence goaded the man higher.

"Just six?" he pleaded, then glumly handed over the heirloom.

Dix quickly scratched out a ticket for the resigned but forlorn customer, and passed it over the counter along with the five pence.

As he exited the shop, the customer cursed, "Blast you, Dix! You and yer shop, you pissant!"

Unaffected, Dix swung a portion of the counter up and away. He jerked his head for Lindsey and Louise to step through. They followed him into a gloomy back room set up as a sort of parlor, the principal adornment of which was a gigantic safe built into the wall. This dim space, where he communed with his gains, was, no doubt, where he met also those customers not receivable in the front of the shop, the rogues who slithered instead through the side door to dispose of stolen goods.

There was only one chair other than the one that time had molded to fit Dix's withering frame. Lindsey offered the remaining chair to Louise, who willingly dropped into it.

"How is it you came by my name?" Dix asked of Louise.

"You are well-known and highly regarded among your contemporaries," she flattered him, "at least the ones we have visited so far."

The pawnbroker showed an array of brown teeth like tiny shattered gravestones. It did not seem like he'd practiced the expression much, as the creases in his face didn't quite fold that way.

"What makes you think that I have such a revolver in my shop?"

"You've brought us back here," replied Louise. "Before that, I merely suspected. Now I'm certain."

"I invite many people into my office," Dix said with a regal sweep of his hand.

"You suggested you could find the revolver we seek for a price," Louise said, "but it's obvious you seldom venture from this building. You work here, you live upstairs, and you have your necessities delivered, the evidence of which surrounds us. Your pallor reinforces those self-evident conclusions. Since you are confident you can lay your hands on this specific revolver model, it must be here."

The pawnbroker reached under the desk, drew forth a Colt Navy revolver, and slammed it to his desk with a menacing thud, the barrel pointed directly at Louise, the chambers clearly loaded. Lindsey flinched; Louise did not bat an eye. "It's yours for fifty pounds," declared Dix, leaning back in his chair.

"I'll not bargain with you, sir, for I will surely lose. You correctly sense that we are in desperate need of a Colt Navy, but our desperation is not so great that we will part with fifty pounds. We would sooner settle for a Remington, and one of those I can readily obtain at a reasonable price."

Unwavering, Dix maintained his smug air.

"Very well, then," said Louise, rising from her chair and turning for the door. "Good day to you, Mr. Dix."

Lindsey followed her. Only when they were half out of the front door did the pawnbroker finally speak up.

"It's not for sale in any case," he shouted from the back room. "Let's discuss your rental proposition. Lock that door so we won't be disturbed."

Louise closed the door, turned the key in the lock, and returned to the back office, Lindsey in tow. Louise retook the chair. Lindsey crossed his arms and said, "Well?"

"Three thousand percent," Dix demanded.

"As I previously stated," replied Louise calmly, "I'll not bargain with you. My astoundingly generous offer remains. You may accept it if you wish. We propose to rent the Colt for one month, for which we will pay you twice the market value of the weapon, which is three pounds. I base that value on my recent investigation of the matter. We will therefore pay you six pounds, a monthly interest rate of two hundred percent of its value. That is an annual interest rate of twenty-four hundred percent."

"More, if I insist on compounding the interest."

"Indeed it would be more, but my offer is for a non-compounded rate of twenty-four hundred percent."

Dix let fewer than three seconds pass before saying, "I will want fifty pounds collateral, else you could choose never to return it, and transform a lucrative rental into a disappointing sale."

"I understand," said Louise. "I will provide collateral, but I cannot give fifty pounds in cash. Even if I could, I would not.

"What will you give me instead?" Dix asked. He thrummed his yellow fingertips together expectantly.

"I will give you my word," said Louise. "That is worth far more to me than any of my meager possessions."

Dix let loose a laugh that concluded in another fit of wet coughing. "As much as all that then, young lady? Such generosity!"

Louise added, "And a handshake, if you wish."

"Why should I trust your word above jewelry?"

"Because I have no jewelry worth fifty pounds. Because you know people, and you know of what they are capable. Look at me, Mr. Dix. Study me. Am I capable of reneging on my word?"

He narrowed his gaze at her and she did not look away. Dust motes drifted between them, illuminated by what light made its way through the dingy office window. At long last he said, "I will take you at your word, Miss—"

"Hawkins," Louise said. "Louise Hawkins. And this is David Lindsey, owner and editor of the *Bristol North Star.*"

Lindsey extended his hand, but Jacob Dix only said, "Never heard of it."

"Well, ah, we're a young newspaper," Lindsey explained, still holding out his hand. "We're just getting started."

Dix leaned back to resume negotiations with Louise. "Circumstances beyond your control might prevent you from keeping your word. The revolver could be stolen, for example, or seized by the police. I must have protection against such an eventuality. Therefore, should you fail to return the revolver within a month, you will pay me a penalty of forty-four pounds. It will be as if you purchased the weapon for fifty pounds, as I initially proposed. Do you agree?"

"It is a very clever arrangement you propose, sir," said Louise. "I would gladly accept if I could. I cannot, however, for I do not have forty-four pounds to my name."

"I will stand good for the penalty," offered Lindsey. "You can take me on my word."

"From you," said Dix, scowling, "I will require a surety bond. You will be needing cartridges, Miss Hawkins. I have just what you need. And, for you, priced at a mere five pounds."

"That's very generous of you, sir, but I expect I will do far better elsewhere."

The pawnbroker's face crackled into a grin. "Yes, Miss Hawkins. I believe you will."

chapter eleven
IN A CLEARING BESIDE CHURCHDOWN LANE

FRIDAY MORNING, 21 MARCH 1879
EASTGATE MARKET, EASTGATE STREET
GLOUCESTER, ENGLAND

The Great Midlands train from Bristol had braked to a stop at the Gloucester Central Station at 9 a.m., neither a minute early nor a minute late. By 9:14, Lindsey and Louise had managed to hail a four-wheeler and load their luggage. Despite the cab's substantial size, the driver had whisked his fare through the throng of farmers, vendors, customers, horses, wagons, and competing cabs to deliver them to the grand entrance of the Eastgate Market. Louise, who had graduated to a single crutch, descended from the cab on her own, carrying two umbrellas. She watched as Lindsey paid the driver before saddling himself with his camera, his tripod, and an obviously heavy portmanteau laden with lens, photographic plates, revolver, and cartridges. The cab pulled away.

They stood side by side before the market that predated even the Norman Conquest. For centuries, it had been held outdoors, but not in its current incarnation. The Eastgate before them occupied a magnificent arcade. Inside, they hoped to obtain six pigs' heads, which they would then transport to Barnwood House Hospital. To Louise's utter surprise, Jeremy had insisted on guiding them through their shooting experiments.

Lindsey slogged into the market without paying the least attention to its entrance, but Louise paused long enough to study the Corinthian portico. High above her was a large clock, reading 9:37 AM, supported by two carved figures. On the right was Father Time, the one who will eventually claim us all, at his leisure or on a whim. On the left was Ceres, the Roman goddess of agriculture, grain crops, fertility, and motherly relationships. Beneath them ran the inscription *The Earth is the Lords and the Fulness Thereof.* Tutting its lack of an apostrophe, Louise stepped through.

The arcade was divided into three spacious bays, each large enough to handle the multitude of stalls, the swarms of people, and the tangle of hand carts transporting endless goods from wagons outside. The bay on the left specialized in vegetables, particularly corn, various grains, and a smattering of fruit. The center dealt in poultry, both alive and butchered. The bay on the right was the one of interest to them, specializing as it did in other butchered meat.

"I propose you wait out front with the gear," suggested Lindsey. "Time is running short, and I'll need to move quickly."

Louise conceded the point. Her right shoulder, under which the crutch resided, had come to bother her far more than her ankle, and sitting seemed preferable to a long walk. Together they passed back through the portico and spied an empty iron bench. Lindsey arrived there first and unburdened himself of equipment.

"Remember," Louise said, "we want pigs with the most upright foreheads that you can find, preferably Gloucestershire Old Spots or Middle Whites, or Plum Puddings in a pinch. Six of them, all of the same breed and size."

"I'll do my best," said Lindsey, turning to leave.

"Under no conditions should you settle for a Tamworth or a Large Black. No sloping foreheads."

"I'll do my best," repeated Lindsey, obviously eager to get to the task at hand.

"Thank you, David," she said sincerely, dropping the last pretense of formality between the two of them. "I couldn't do this without you."

He nodded, turned, and disappeared into the crowded market.

Louise examined the bench, taking particular note of the backrest: an array of metallic ferns, ornate to be sure, but a poor imitation of Coalbrookdale. The bench would properly support her, though, so she settled onto it for a wait of un-known length, pondering the vast array of foods beyond the gate, and observing the people who provided and benefit-ted from such a cornucopia. Her mind soon drifted from the crowd, and she shuddered at the circumstances that caused her to be sitting beneath two carved figures of life and death. It was Ceres who provided the bounty. It was Father Time who carried away those who would benefit from the abundance, just as he had carried away William Perenna with that gunshot wound. What was it about that wound that Jeremy could see but she could not? What would they learn from shooting dead pigs in the forehead?

She longed for the time when she could visit a market and purchase barley and chicken without a care, then chided her-self for her self-centeredness. She pondered the adventure that had once filled her with an inappropriate sense of ex-citement, but now threatened to overwhelm her with feelings of sadness, dread, and foreboding. Anna Perenna's trial grew imminent, and the outcome could not currently be doubted, unjust as it might be.

For more than an hour she allowed her mind to dance from thought to thought, with no sense of direction and no resolution. Lindsey broke into her musing with a loud "Hello!" from atop a four-wheeled wagon complete with headboard, sideboards, and tailboard, drawn by a farm horse in fine fettle, and driven by a wholesome lad obviously accustomed to fieldwork. Lindsey and the young farmhand jumped down to heft the photographic gear and the port-manteau into the back.

"The boy comes with the wagon," Lindsey explained, strug-gling to help Louise aboard with an awkwardly placed hand, prompting an assist from the lad. "The owner would rent me the wagon only if I hired his son as my driver. It's the farmer's way of ensuring his wagon's return and making a few extra coins to boot."

"Does he know it may come back with bullet holes?" asked Louise, settling herself on the bench.

"Not only does he know about it," said Lindsey, "but at a penny a hole, he tingled at the thought."

The farmer's son clambered up and settled in the center, next to Louise. She took the opportunity to introduce herself.

"I'm Louise Hawkins," she said. "Thank you for your assistance."

"MacGregor, miss," the lad mumbled, touching the brim of his hat as if to doff it without actually doing so.

Lindsey circled and climbed aboard on the driver's opposite side. MacGregor jostled the reins and the mare made her way deftly through the crowd towards Northgate Street. Louise turned to examine the pigs' heads in the bed of the wagon. There were just five, one short of what Jeremy had instructed: three Old Spots, one Middle White, and one Plum Pudding.

"It was the best I could do," said Lindsey, shrugging. "And I was lucky to get them. They're from four different vendors, and this wagon is from a fifth. I assure you that when I started my own newspaper, I did not anticipate being tasked with purchasing six identical pigs' heads, each having a specific skull structure. I've done my level best."

"An excellent selection," said Louise. "Nicely done. Thank you once again."

Lindsey nodded, mollified by her words. MacGregor guided the farm horse along Northgate Street, which transitioned to London Road, which curved onto Barnwood Road. They traveled slowly, so more than half an hour passed before MacGregor, with a twitch of the reins, turned them onto the broad path that led to the Barnwood House Hospital front entrance.

"I'll fetch Jeremy," said Louise, as the wagon squeaked and clattered to rest. Jeremy appeared on his own, though, and Louise realized that he must have been watching for them, either excited by the prospect of spending time with her, or anxious at being around Lindsey. Probably some of each, she decided. Without a word or sidelong glance, he walked directly to the wagon and climbed effortlessly over the sideboards into the back. He plumped up a reasonably clean sailcloth and settled onto it, facing the rear.

"You don't have to sit back there," offered Lindsey, hoping to kindle a friendship. "You can have my spot. I'll sit in back."

"I'm fine here," Jeremy responded flatly. "Louise and I were born on a farm. She was too young to remember, but I recall those days fondly. I'm perfectly comfortable back here with these pigs, even though there are but five and they are of three different breeds."

Lindsey slumped as Jeremy curtly addressed the driver. "Return to the main road, turn right, continue to the first road on your left. That's Churchdown Lane. Follow it deep into the woods."

The carthorse lurched into her measured, persistent plod. She turned when directed by subtle pressure on her reins, and turned again not long thereafter. The smooth, hardened lane gave way to a rutted pathway. That narrowed to nearly nothing as they emerged into a broad, sunny clearing. Easing along for a few steps, the horse came to a standstill and stretched her neck for some nice grass just within reach.

***

FRIDAY AFTERNOON, 21 MAY 1879
A CLEARING BESIDE CHURCHDOWN LANE
BARNWOOD, ENGLAND

The wagon's passengers leapt into action.

Jeremy vaulted the right-hand sideboards and assisted Louise to the ground. Lindsey retrieved his portmanteau from beneath the bench, having MacGregor hand it down to him after alighting. The farmhand followed him, unhitched and led the mare to a lush, grassy spot in the shade of the forest's edge, where he hobbled her and allowed her to graze. He sat against a sweet chestnut tree to observe the antics of the strange people paying him handsomely for this, an entire day free of labor, plus free entertainment.

Jeremy hefted the right-hand sideboards from the wagon and leaned them against its gate. He reached across the bed, dragged each of the five pigs' heads to the edge and spaced them evenly apart along the length of the right side. Using small chunks of wood and other detritus, he supported each of the heads in the position he desired, foreheads nearly vertical. He paced off fifteen steps from the wagon and dragged a short line in the grass, digging down to the dirt with his heel, then turned and announced, "We'll shoot from here."

Lindsey placed his camera and tripod equipment ten yards distant, well out of the line of fire. He returned to retrieve the luggage as Louise hobbled to Jeremy's side. Portmanteau in hand, Lindsey halted at her right, the three of them standing in a row, staring at five severed pigs' heads. MacGregor maintained his relaxed repose under the tree. The mare pulled at the grass contentedly, nearly as happy as her master, though bothered by more flies.

Louise turned to Jeremy. "Thank you for coming along."

"I don't want you killed," he stated.

"I assume you don't want *anyone* killed," she offered, nodding subtly towards Lindsey. When Jeremy said nothing in reply, she added, "Well, thank you for whatever reason you came."

He held out his hand towards Lindsey, insisting without words that Lindsey hand over the portmanteau. From the hefty bag, Jeremy took Dix's revolver, half-cocked the trigger, turned the cylinder to satisfy himself than none of the chambers was loaded, examined the weapon's markings, then presented it flat in his upturned palm.

"We have a Colt 1851 Navy percussion revolver, thirty-six caliber, serial number thirteen sixteen. Assuming the autopsy report is accurate, this weapon is essentially the same as that which discharged the bullet that penetrated the skull of Lt. William Perenna. There are no cartridges in the chambers and there are no percussion caps on the nipples. Nonetheless, I will not point it at anyone upon whom I do not intend to fire, and each of you will, if I allow you to handle it, treat it with equal caution, keeping it always aimed downrange, in the direction you intend to shoot. Fail do so and you will sit over there with the young driver, who finds this all very amusing."

Lindsey and Louise nodded.

"Mr. Lindsey, confirm what I just told you."

"I am never to point this gun—"

"ANY GUN!" Jeremy shouted, his voice reverberating through the trees. A trio of sparrows flitted away in fright, and Lindsey nearly stumbled backwards.

"I am never to point any gun at anyone unless—"

"Anyone, including yourself."

"Very well," Lindsey croaked. "I am never to point any gun at anyone, including myself, unless I intend to shoot that person."

"Louise, now you," Jeremy said, only slightly mollified.

"I am never to point any gun at anyone, including myself, unless I intend to shoot him—or her."

Jeremy squared himself to the wagon, spread his feet, and raised the Colt. Grasping its handle with his right hand, steadying his right with his left, he rested his right index finger along the trigger guard.

"This revolver requires two separate actions to fire it," he said, focusing on his target. "First, the shooter must cock the hammer all the way back, like this."

Without relaxing his grip, he used his right thumb to pull the hammer back to its fully cocked position. As he pulled the hammer back, the cylinder rotated clockwise, aligning the next chamber with the barrel.

"Now that the weapon is cocked, it may be fired by pulling the trigger."

He closed one eye, sighted along the barrel, placed his right index finger on the trigger, and pulled. The hammer dropped with an unimpressive click. He lowered the weapon, pointing it at the ground ahead of him.

"Had that cylinder been loaded, the hammer would have struck a percussion cap covering this nipple at the back of the chamber. The percussion cap would have ignited, sending its flame through the hole in the nipple, igniting the gunpowder inside the chamber. That gunpowder would have then exploded, converting itself to high temperature, high pressure, expanding gas, forcing the bullet out of the chamber, accelerating it through the barrel, forcing it from the muzzle with sufficient kinetic energy to wreak catastrophic harm on any living soul within its range. Do you understand?"

Lindsey and Louise nodded.

Jeremy pursed his lips.

"I understand," said Louise first, and Lindsey echoed her.

Keeping the weapon pointed downrange, Jeremy held it towards Lindsey. "Now you, Mr. Lindsey. You practice firing it. And you, dear sister, please give him your place."

Louise stepped back to where she could watch. Lindsey took Louise's vacated position, nervously taking the revolver by its handle. Being careful to keep the weapon pointed away from him, he raised it and attempted to emulate what Jeremy had showed them.

"NO!" barked Jeremy, yanking the gun away from him. "You're going to blow your finger off. I showed you how to hold it: left hand around right fingers, like this. Both hands around the handle, do you see?"

Lindsey nodded, sheepishly.

"Do you see this gap?" Jeremy asked, pointing to the slender, almost invisible space between the front of the cylinder and the beginning of the barrel. "It is a necessary evil. Without it, the cylinder couldn't rotate. But some of the gunpowder blast escapes from here. That side blast is energetic and scorching hot. If you extend your finger over this gap, as you just did, and if you are lucky, you'll merely sear the flesh off the bone. If you get what you deserve for being so foolish, you'll lose the finger. Do you understand?"

Lindsey blinked and nodded, thoroughly chastened.

"Not good enough. Tell me that you understand what will happen and why."

"I understand that if I fire with my finger near the cylinder gap, I will be scorched or maimed."

"Good. Now hold the weapon correctly," Jeremy demanded.

Lindsey accepted the revolver and corrected his grip. Jeremy automatically reached to adjust Lindsey's fingers, then suddenly withdrew before touching them, and simply pointed to the flaws in the grip.

"Keep your right index finger free, resting alongside the trigger guard. Good. Don't cover this thumb, because you're going to use it to cock the hammer. Close your left eye. Align the weapon such that this groove, here, aligns with both this front sight, here, and the pig's head, over there, the centermost one. Let me know when you have everything in line."

"All right," said Lindsey, attempting to follow all the instructions. "I have them aligned, but not steadily. The gun keeps moving."

"Only because you keep moving," said Jeremy. "You move, the gun follows. When we get around to actually firing a bullet, I assure you that the weapon will then move and your hands will follow. For now, just hold it as steadily as you can. Now reach up with your right thumb and cock the hammer."

Lindsey did as instructed, resetting his aim afterwards.

"Now place your right index finger on the trigger, but don't pull."

Lindsey did.

"Now pull the trigger."

The hammer clicked.

"More gently next time," Jeremy instructed. "Now, do that twenty-five times more."

Lindsey turned his head in surprise, half-expecting his instructor to be smiling at his own joke.

"We have a great deal left to do," said Jeremy. "We're going to lose daylight if you just stand there peering at me. Get on with it, or go sit by the horse and driver."

During the next several minutes, Lindsey practiced firing the revolver with Jeremy insisting on minor corrections along the way. Jeremy then took the revolver from Lindsey and instructed Louise in the same matter-of-fact fashion and tone, though without once raising his voice.

"Now lower the weapon," he ordered her, taking a box of cartridges from the portmanteau. He read the label aloud. "'Six combustible envelope cartridges, made of Hazard's powder, either for Colt's or Remington's revolving belt pistols. Thirty-six caliber. Warranted superior quality.' Good choice."

He removed one cartridge and one percussion cap from the box. He held up the cartridge for his students to behold.

"Death wrapped in paper," he said. "Twenty-five grains of gunpowder and an eighty-grain, pure lead, round ball bullet.

The gunpowder is a mixture of seventy-five percent saltpeter, fifteen percent charcoal, and ten percent brimstone, also known as sulfur. When ignited by this percussion cap—" He held the tiny cylindrical object to the end of the larger cartridge "—fifty percent of the powder will be converted to high pressure, high temperature, expanding gases. The resulting solids will be obvious as a cloud of white smoke and, less noticeable, as black residue within the revolver's chamber and barrel. Depending on how keen your senses, the smoke may smell of charcoal and, more surprisingly, leave a hint of steaming brimstone on your tongue and palate."

He paused, regarding the percussion cap, before venturing into poetic abstraction.

"Fire and brimstone," he announced. "A perfect metaphor for a weapon such as the one you are about to get a taste of."

Having their rapt attention, he took the revolver from Louise and pointed it upward.

"You load all the cartridges you intend to fire from the front of the cylinder before adding even a single percussion cap to the rear."

He pulled the trigger slowly to its half-cocked position, which allowed him to rotate the cylinder freely. He inserted the cartridge as far as it would easily go, and then rotated the cylinder to align the partially loaded chamber with the long rod running along the bottom of the barrel. Pulling the rod drove a shorter ramrod against the cartridge, pushing it deeper into the chamber.

"Since I am only going to fire a single round this time, I can now install the percussion cap."

Pointing the revolver at a forty-five degree angle to the ground in front of him, he pushed the open end of the percussion cap over the nipple behind the loaded chamber, and then rotated that chamber to the ten o'clock position. He pulled the trigger slightly, and then lowered the hammer to rest at the top of the cylinder, between two chambers.

"The next time the trigger is pulled back," he said, "the loaded chamber will rotate into the firing position. The weapon will be but a trigger-pull away from launching death and destruction from its muzzle."

"Who taught you?" asked Lindsey.

"Father," said Jeremy, without affect.

"But I understand him to have been aged and blind," said Lindsey.

Louise tensed. Jeremy raised the revolver towards the wagon and offered it to Lindsey.

"He was never so old not to have his wits about him," Jeremy said, "and never so blind not to recall vision sufficient to teach me."

"I'm sorry," said Lindsey, abashed. "That came out wrong."

"Be extra careful," Jeremy said. "It's loaded and it's lethal."

Lindsey gripped the revolver.

"Let's see if you can put a bullet in the pig's forehead. Keep the weapon aimed out there, and maybe you won't kill anyone. Hold it correctly and maybe you won't blow your finger off. Do as I've instructed, and you might hit a pig, perhaps even the one you were aiming at, but I doubt it. The result of your next trigger pull will be very different from your practice firings. It will be loud. The weapon will kick back and upwards. Don't let go of it. And whatever you do, don't lose your head and wheel around afterwards, pointing somewhere you oughtn't. Do you understand?"

"I understand," Lindsey replied, repeating all of Jeremy's specifics to his instructor's satisfaction.

Jeremy nodded, then stepped back, motioning for Louise to do the same.

"And you understand," Lindsey added, taking aim, "that I might surprise you."

"That'll be the day," Jeremy said, with a smirk.

The revolver discharged with an awesome crack, a burst of flame, and a cloud of smoke. The recoil jerked Lindsey's arms upwards. He staggered back a step, or tried to, but caught his heel on something otherwise insignificant in the grass, and fell backwards. Going down, he kept the revolver pointed away from himself and everyone else, landing flat on his back, arms still extended, the empty revolver trained at the cerulean sky. He lay there, breathing heavily, aiming towards the heavens, afraid to move. Louise took a step towards him but Jeremy barricaded her with an arm even as he joined MacGregor in laughter. The farm boy clutched his stomach and collapsed to one side of the tree trunk. Jeremy doubled over, supporting himself with a hand on a knee. It was the first time Lindsey had heard him laugh.

Finally composing himself, Jeremy pried the revolver from Lindsey's hands. "I'll admit I was wrong about you, Mr. Lindsey. I scoffed when you suggested it, but you certainly did surprise me. Never would I have anticipated such a performance."

"I hit the pig?" Lindsey asked in dazed astonishment.

"Perhaps one in the next county," chuckled Jeremy, "but certainly none here."

Lindsey's arms fell to his sides. He gazed into the sky as if hoping to catch sight of his last shred of dignity as it flew away. The phlegmatic carthorse snorted as it continued grazing. Only Louise seemed to empathize with him.

"I have the weapon now," said Jeremy, "so feel free to right yourself. I can't imagine how you might, in the process, injure anyone other than yourself."

MacGregor's laughter subsided only after Lindsey regained his feet. Jeremy returned to the portmanteau for another cartridge and percussion cap, which he loaded before presenting the revolver to Louise. "Let's see if you can do better."

Louise accepted the weapon without the slightest hesitation, assumed the shooting stance absorbed from Lindsey's tutorial, grasped the revolver as he had, peeked behind her to make sure the ground was even and clear, turned back to the target, raised the weapon, shifted her weight ever so slightly towards her toes, took aim, and applied gentle pressure to the trigger, pulling it slowly, ever so slowly, until—

A flash and a crack split the air, and another cloud of smoke arose.

Louise's arms jerked slightly. She rocked back just a bit, but managed to stand her ground. She brought the gun back down to its firing position.

"You can open your eyes now," Jeremy told her.

Other than having been recently deprived of a body, she saw her target unharmed. A small round hole, though, had appeared in the sideboard behind the pig, slightly above and to the right.

Jeremy stepped over and took the revolver from her. He began loading six fresh cartridges into the gun. "Not as entertaining as Mr. Lindsey's effort, but not bad."

He took up a firing stance entirely different from that he'd just taught his students, standing instead almost sideward to the target, his right foot in front, toes pointed straight ahead, his left foot in back, planted perpendicular.

"We're going to run out of daylight," he said, placing his left fist on his hip, "so I'll expedite matters." He raised the Colt with a rigid right arm. "It has taken us a while, but you have each already learned something of considerable value about the case, though you fail yet to realize it." He cocked the weapon, sighted, and fired. The recoil jarred his arm just slightly, but the remainder of him stood rigid and unmoved. A round hole appeared in the center of the leftmost pig's forehead.

Lindsey and Louise stared in awe at the bullet hole.

Jeremy repositioned himself closer to the wagon. "That shot was from fifteen feet. This one will be from ten."

He raised the revolver, cocked it, took aim, and fired. A hole appeared in the forehead of the second pig.

"This one will be from five."

He fired. Another hole, this one in the center target.

"Now it might get interesting," he said, closing to nearly touching the fourth pig's pale forehead. "From six inches."

He fired. Because he obscured the view of the target, neither Louise nor Jeremy could see the result. They could only see Jeremy looking down at his midsection. With the revolver pointed at the ground, he turned towards them. His white shirt was spattered with blood and bits of disgusting matter.

Louise yelped, running to him.

"It's not mine," he said. "It's from the pig. It must have splashed from the entry wound. Look!"

Louise examined the hole above the pig's eyes. Lindsey advanced and peered over her shoulder. There was a wound, to be sure, but rather than neat and round, its edges were a bit ragged, surrounded by a ring of small dark spots and a broader band of fine soot. The shot had burst out the back of the pig's skull, and spattered the wagon bed with gore.

"Now we have learned two things about the case. First, Anna Perenna did not shoot her husband from six inches distant."

"Because she didn't have his blood on her clothes," said Louise.

"And because there was not this speckled ring surrounding his entry wound," added Lindsey.

"Correct, both of you. And it is unlikely that she shot him from a distance."

"Because the entry wound was not round," continued Lindsey, "It was more ragged, like this one."

Louise completed the thought. "And because she would have been unable to hit him in the forehead, just as Lindsey and I weren't practiced enough to hit our targets at all."

"Precisely," said Jeremy. "Now you can appreciate why I came here with you. It was not just to keep you safe, but also to have you demonstrate for yourselves the improbability of her shooting him from across the room. I expected you both to miss, but I didn't anticipate ruining my shirt. This is most interesting."

"Maybe she had been trained to shoot," Lindsey speculated.

"Perhaps," said Jeremy. "You're the reporter; you should know."

"I believe she could have shot him from five feet away," said Louise, her hand to her chest, feeling her heart racing. "Even I would have hit him from that distance."

"Even if you had never fired the weapon? Even if you had never received any instruction? Even if you had never before held a revolver in your hand? Even if you were pregnant, and angry, filled with righteous, murderous intent?"

She thought for a moment before conceding. "Probably not so squarely in the forehead. So where do we go from here?"

"You two stand back," Jeremy said, "so that I may remove my shirt and take two additional shots. Then Lindsey must take his photographs before we lose the light."

"Why—"

"We can talk while the plates are being exposed. Now, please, step back." Placing the revolver on the wagon's platform, Jeremy shed his shirt, explaining, "If there's more blood to come, I don't want it confused with this mess."

It had clearly been many years since the skin of Jeremy's arms or torso had seen the light of day, and his pallor stood in notable contrast even to the fairness of his face and hands. He laid his shirt on the wagon, careful not to smear the spatter on its front. Louise noticed a long, aged scar on his back, a degree whiter still than the skin surrounding it. The wound must have been shallow, she realized, since the scar was puckered and raised above the adjoining skin. It had not been there when they were children, and he had never spoken to her of such a wounding. Questions arose within her, but she doubted they would ever be answered.

Jeremy waved Louise and Lindsey further back, raised the revolver, placed its muzzle firmly to the forehead of the last pig, and then pulled the trigger. The blast was slightly muffled, compared to the earlier gunshots, but the damage done was far more substantial. Jeremy stepped back, revealing to the others a gaping starburst wound in the pigskin, and a wagon bed further spattered with gore.

"As I expected," said Jeremy.

"Just like Perenna's," Louise observed. "How did you know?"

Jeremy inspected his chest for blood, and, seeing but little, moved to more closely examine the last pig.

"I think the damage is much more serious when the muzzle is in contact with the skin," he said, "because the hot, expanding gases follow the ball into the wound. Hence the wound edges tear and gape. Some of that gas rushes back out, ripping the skin into these triangles that radiate from the center. I pondered the problem for hours after you last left. I put myself in the place of the bullet, of the expanding gas, and of the skin, one after the other, asking at each point how I would respond. It was a three-pipe problem, I assure you of that. Stand clear for one last shot."

Rather than aiming at the pig's head, he held the Colt alongside it, nearly touching, before firing into the opposite sideboard.

"As I expected," he said, pointing to the dead animal's temple. A dark smudge could now be seen. "This testing has satisfied me that my working hypothesis was correct. Examine the evidence yourself. The case is solved. Even a bumbling police detective would not dare deny this evidence."

Louise and Lindsey raced forward to examine the most recent result.

"Set up your camera, Mr. Lindsey." His words seemed to drag. Suddenly he sounded like a London gin hound fresh from a night at the tavern. "You need to photograph this, all of it. My sshirt, the pigsh, all of it. Shtart wish the final—"

Jeremy fell to the ground, convulsing.

———✦———

Friday afternoon, 21 March 1879
A clearing beside Churchdown Lane,
Barnwood, England

The mare grazed contentedly, but her master, sitting beneath the sweet chestnut tree, was unsettled by this turn of his leisurely afternoon. The tallest of his passengers had suddenly stiffened and collapsed, then began to violently twitch. The woman hurried to roll him onto his side. She sat down in the grass with his head in her lap. She stroked his hair even as he spasmed. All the while, the small man stood frozen in place. The incident lasted several minutes, and then stopped as suddenly as it had started. The afflicted man remained obviously out of sorts. He groaned and mumbled until he fell asleep, his head still in the woman's lap, his spittle falling on her dress.

MacGregor realized in a flash that the tall man was not an employee of the hospital, but a patient. All three of them, however, must certainly be insane: guns and blood and severed heads. His entertaining afternoon took on a more sinister complexion.

"He'll sleep now," said Louise to Lindsey. "A half hour, perhaps longer. I assume you can take your photographs and load the wagon without my assistance. It will be best if we leave soon after he awakens."

Lindsey was still considerably rattled, having never before witnessed an epileptic seizure.

"Will he be all right?"

"He will have a splitting headache, but it will pass."

"He'll be all right, though?"

"He is already all right," said Louise. "This is as much a part of him as his brilliance."

Lindsey turned, seemed a little startled to find his camera close at hand, then at last set up to photograph the fifth pig's head. With a glimpse at his pocket watch, he removed the lens cap.

"He experiences these fits once each week?" he asked.

"On average. He could have another before we get him back to Barnwood. He might not have another for a month. They are not predictable, but, as I mentioned before, he is working on a mathematical means of making them so."

Lindsey replaced the cap, swapped the exposed plate for a fresh one, and began a second, longer exposure of the same pig's forehead.

"Can he tell when they are about to occur?"

"He tells me that sometimes a strange sensation comes over him beforehand. *An aura* he calls it, but it comes too late for him to react."

"Is he aware of what is happening to him when the seizures take hold?"

"He'll have no memory of the seizure itself. He'll slowly regain his senses and, at some point, realize that he's had another fit. He'll look around to see where he is and, more importantly to him, who has witnessed his seizure. Now that you have seen him seize, he will shy away from you. He'll feel humiliated."

"He has no reason to," said Lindsey over his shoulder, setting up to photograph the side of the pig's head.

"But he will," said Louise quietly.

"He didn't care much for me in the first place," Lindsey said

"If he hadn't taken to you, he wouldn't have spent the time teaching you to shoot properly. He would have just taken all the shots himself, and we would have learned less than we have."

"You speak of his feelings in the past tense," observed Lindsey, "I assume you mean that he will feel differently about me now."

He replaced the lens cap and began swapping plates as Louise responded.

"Yes, everything has changed. Before, he was in command. You relied on him for your safety and insight into the case. Now his wits and capabilities have been taken from him, if only temporarily, and he relies instead on us for his well being. You can certainly see that."

Lindsey's face collapsed into a veritable theater mask of sadness. He removed the lens cap, beginning his third exposure of the residue on the side of the fifth pig's head.

"And if he sees you looking at him like that, it will only make matters worse. He doesn't need pity, but for people to accept him as he is, with his afflictions alongside his wonders."

As Lindsey moved his camera to the next pig's head in line, he noticed Louise looking at the scar on Jeremy's back. She ran her finger along it without touching.

"What happened?" he asked.

"I don't know," said Louise, without looking up.

"Are you curious?"

"Frightfully so."

"Are you going to ask?"

She pondered her response. Looking Lindsey in the eye, she said, "We all have secrets we don't want anyone else to know, don't we?"

He straightened. A thoughtful expression spread over his face. He considered Louise and Jeremy for a long moment before replying. "Yes. We all do."

chapter twelve

ALONE

Jeremy stormed into his room. He threw himself into one of the chairs at the table, yanked a journal from the collection opposite, and turned to the last page with writing on it. From a nearby pile, he grabbed a sheet of foolscap and slammed it on the table, as hard as one might slam a piece of paper. He jerked an Eagle Gold pencil from its holder and sharpened it with a vengeance.

Louise followed him without knocking, settling quietly into the chair beside him. She watched shavings pour from the cheap Spencer sharpener that she had purchased for him long ago, when he needed something in lieu of a knife—a possession forbidden of patients. She had hoped ever since to buy him a Webster sharpener, with its ingenious rotating handle, but Jeremy would have to make do with the Spencer for a bit longer.

After running his fingers over his last journal entry, scanning as he went, Jeremy began scratching numbers on the foolscap but almost immediately snapped his pencil lead. He resharpened the pencil, then managed to pierce the paper with it. He wadded the paper and hurled it across the room, where it fell near a wicker waste paper basket. He jerked another sheet from the stack and began anew, this time a bit more cautiously.

He settled into a rhythm, scratching barely legible mathematical calculations on the foolscap and adding precisely penned entries into his journal. Louise remained still beside him.

Three quarters of an hour passed. Finally calm, he spoke in a near whisper, not meeting her eyes. "You'll miss the last train."

"I've already missed it," she replied. "Lindsey departed immediately after dropping us off. He had to return the wagon and get back to Bristol. He still has a newspaper to run. And a family."

"And I have a universal constant to calculate."

The siblings sat quietly for a while longer.

"I'm calm now," Jeremy said at last, "and I would like to be left to my calculations, please. They'll find a room for you in guest quarters."

"I need your help," she said, almost under her breath.

"No you don't," he replied. "You saw the evidence. You know she didn't shoot him. You know who did. I have nothing else to offer you, except perhaps my self-pity."

"I need you to convince them," she persisted. "They'll not listen to me."

"Because of your sex, your womanhood? Have John do it then."

"He's in Ventnor. Mother fetched him yesterday. He's not well."

"So it has settled on him again," said Jeremy, slumping in his chair, pausing to ponder the mortal implications. When he returned his attention to Louise, he was somewhat less harsh.

"Have Lindsey convince them. The journalist has the power of the press."

"Lindsey and I both spent most of Wednesday trying to talk to Anna Perenna's solicitor and her barrister. We explained how it was quite impossible for her to have shot her husband. I tried to detail the measurements that we made at the house, and show them my calculations that proved the angles all wrong. Had she shot him, the bullet hole in the wall would have been higher, just as you anticipated it would be. The numbers were all there. They would have none of it, though. They said

I came to them too late, and that it would be too confusing for a jury. As a scientific witness, they tell me, I am incompetent, and the court will refuse to hear me."

"Why would you think that anyone, anyone at all, would be interested in your numbers, or your facts, or your logic? People are emotional creatures, not rational beings. We instinctively choose our beliefs based on what comforts us, rejecting facts and arguments that challenge those comforting beliefs."

"Lindsey told them we were going to shoot bullets into pigs' heads, that we hoped the testing would provide even more evidence of her innocence."

"And how did that work out?" asked Jeremy, amused for the first time since Lindsey's wild shot.

"They laughed at us." Jeremy's amusement faded as he took in the strain in her voice. "They told us that no judge in this or any other county would allow testimony about pigs' heads to be presented to jurymen in a murder trial. Mr. Lindsey explained that he would take photographs. They laughed even harder. They told us to come back when our results had been published in *The Lancet*, and they bid us a good day."

"They can't claim self-defense," said Jeremy, "so I suspect they will try accident, or *non compos mentis*. Given that she refuses to speak, I expect the latter."

"Yes, the latter," confirmed Louise. "If they fail, as I suspect they will, she will hang. If they succeed, her child will be taken from her and she will be placed in an asylum. Not a private hospital like Barnwood, a *real* one. A public asylum for the poor."

"Better to hang," Jeremy intoned.

"Then you will help me?"

"You don't need me. You have Lindsey."

"Anna Perenna will be tried and convicted on Monday," said Louise. "Lindsey will not have an edition out before the trial. He will be able, afterwards, to report on the inequity of her hanging, but he won't be able to forestall it."

Jeremy tried to get back to his work. "A special edition then."

"And what would that special edition say? That the angles are wrong? That we can divine truth by firing bullets into pigs' heads? I need you, Jeremy. *She* needs you. She needs some-one who understands weapons and the wounds they create. Lindsey can't even hit the side of a wagon, and I'm, I'm—"

"A woman?" Jeremy scoffed. "There you go again! Well, if they won't listen to you because you wear a dress and petticoats, then they certainly won't listen to me as I seize and thrash about on the courtroom floor. I may not fully appreciate the challenges you face as a woman, but you have no idea what it is like to be an epileptic, to have everything you value of yourself randomly stripped away, replaced by a weak simpleton, in public, in front of others—"

He turned back to his work. She noticed glimmers at the corners of his eyes. She had never seen him so close to tears. Barely audible, he added, "I won't do it. I cannot."

A tear dropped onto the paper. He quickly wadded the page, then tore at it and brushed the remnants from the table. He pulled a fresh sheet from the diminishing pile, and set back to calculating.

Louise sat quietly long enough to let her brother compose himself. "She will hang," she said, finally.

"That's not my business," Jeremy replied. "You brought me a seemingly indecipherable mystery. I solved it for you. I've done my part. Take what you've learned to the police, and let them do their business. Then you can return to your sewing and mending and piano playing and whatever else you think women are supposed to do."

"Then you won't help me?"

"Yes I will. This much: don't lecture them, *show* them. That might work. Probably not. That's my advice. That's all I have to offer."

"But you won't come with me?"

"I love you as deeply as any brother can love a sister," he replied as he scribbled, "but I can't always be there for you. This is something that you will have to face without me."

———✦———

EIGHT YEARS EARLIER
WEDNESDAY MORNING, 13 MARCH 1871
SOUTHFIELD COTTAGE, LECKHAMPTON ROAD
LECKHAMPTON, ENGLAND

"Why must I go?" sobbed thirteen-year-old Louise.

"We all must go," replied Jeremy. "The family is blown asunder. We are the blast fragments. Mary and Nem will move back with Father to the farm in Minsterworth. Mother will stay with Aunt Louisa in Whitechurch. You and John will go to school in Clifton. That is the way it will be, and neither you nor I can do anything about it.

"That's so far, so terribly far. Where will you be? Will you be near?"

"I'm being sent to a place called Barnwood House, not too far from here."

"Will you visit me frequently?"

"I'll try. I suspect those who watch over me won't allow it."

"Why not? Because you shake and shiver sometimes? Why should I have to be alone?"

"There will be a score of girls your age living in, and more day students. I understand that Badminton is quite a wonderful school for young women so bright as you."

"I'm thirteen years old! I'll be the youngest. I'll be the newest. I'll be the one they tease. Why can't we all stay together? Why must Mother and Father live apart?"

"This is the way it is going to be, Louise, whether we like it or not."

"So I'll be on my own?" she sobbed.

"Yes," he said, his heart breaking, though he kept a stoic countenance.

chapter thirteen
THE TRIAL

Monday morning, 24 March 1879
The Guildhall, Broad Street
Bristol, England

"There being seven cases before us and twelve petty jurors properly sworn," said Judge Royland Blair, "I call this session of the Bristol Assizes to order. We shall hear the cases in the following order: that of John Skelton, then William Roult, then codefendants Charles Bird and Thomas Groves, followed by the cases of Sallie Mills Alden, Edward Deacon, Anna Perenna, and John Fellows. The jurymen will then retire to render their verdicts. Mr. Heathcote, are you prepared to proceed?"

"We are, my lord," said the prosecutor.

Each of the many men before the bar, both prosecution and defense, was elaborately bewigged, a rolled and pigtailed white hairpiece perched atop his own hair, save one of the defending barristers whose head beneath was as smooth as a duck's egg. The judge's wig was longer and even more elaborate, and only slightly askew.

"John Skelton," said Judge Blair, addressing the pitiful specimen who had just been escorted to the dock, "you have been brought to this court to stand trial for the charge of stealing a pair of boots from Mr. John Hinson of Long Orton. How do you plead?"

"Not guilty, m'lord," said the hunched defendant, in a choked, nearly silent voice.

Thus began the string of trials preceding that of Anna Perenna's. In the first of them, that of John Skelton, the prosecution called as witnesses John Hinson, he of the allegedly purloined boots, and Whitfield Browning, who had witnessed their theft by the defendant. Hinson testified to being at the Red Lion public house, falling asleep, and awakening there in stocking feet. Browning testified that, as he entered the Red Lion, he saw the defendant leaving with a pair of boots in hand. The defendant, in his statement, argued that Browning must certainly be mistaken, for he, John Skelton, had not been in Long Orton on that day. It having been established that the defendant had, within the last seven years, served time in prison, he faced severe punishment. His trial required scarcely more than a quarter of an hour to complete.

William Roult, a laborer of age twenty-five, was then tried for burgling the dwelling of Robert Nicholls and stealing various articles. Again Mr. Heathcote prosecuted, and again the prisoner pleaded not guilty. Unlike the first defendant, Mr. Roult was defended by a barrister, one Mr. Cockerell. This case was one of circumstantial evidence. Nicholls's housekeeper fastened up the home securely that night, and on the following morning found the kitchen door broken open, and several pigs' cheeks, a cutlet of pork, a half loaf of bread, and a piece of cheese missing. Defendant Roult had been seen in the area, and one of his shoes corresponded with footprints found on the premises. The police discovered the stolen food in the tops of some old trees not far from the place of the burglary. This trial lasted fourteen minutes.

Next, expeditiously, Charles Bird and Thomas Groves, butchers in partnership, were charged with sending fouled meat to the London market. Through its witnesses, the prosecution established that the two butchers had dressed and sent to the London market the carcass of a diseased calf, provided to them only for the purpose of feeding their dogs. The prosecution established further that the two defendants had received a pig that had been under the care of a cow doctor for seven weeks. They had been ordered to kill and bury the pig, which had been diagnosed as incurable. While they did indeed kill the pig, they sent the pork along for sale. Their trial lasted forty-one minutes. A few spectators avowed their determination to avoid both pork and beef in the future.

The fourth trial involved a raggedly dressed little girl of eleven years, charged with stealing six shillings from a woman. A bag containing six shillings was found in her possession. When questioned at the scene, the girl admitted to having systematically engaged in picking pockets for the past three years. Proud of her skill, she demonstrated her technique in the presence of the police, emptying the purse of a woman bystander without attracting notice. Sallie Mills Alden's trial lasted nine minutes. She had no defender and nothing to say in her own defense.

In the fifth trial, Edward Deacon, aged twenty-eight, was tried for the murder of his wife. They had been married nine years, had led unhappy lives, and were by all accounts constantly quarrelling. On the twenty-second of February, the prisoner went to a neighbor's house and borrowed a sharp, slender knife, stating that he wanted to whittle some wood. Minutes later the neighbor heard agonized screams that soon declined to a mortal groaning. The neighbor rushed towards the next house and, when she met the defendant along the way, asked him what he had done. He replied, "Go and see." She went in, finding Mrs. Deacon unconscious, on the floor, near death, blood spurting from a slender knife wound on the left side of her neck, blood spilling less rapidly from another wound in her left breast. The neighbor remembered nothing more of consequence since she then swooned, not to regain consciousness until the body had been removed. Dr. Weston testified that both the jugular vein and the carotid artery had been transected, that the immediate cause of death was blood loss through the severed carotid. The judge cut him short when he attempted to explain the difference in fluidic pressure difference between the carotid, which supplied oxygenated blood from the heart to the brain, and the jugular, which carried carbon dioxide laden blood from the brain to the lungs. The trial of Edward Deacon took fifty-one minutes, but would have exceeded an hour had the good doctor been allowed to proceed.

"We now turn to the trial of Anna Perenna," said Judge Blair. "Mr. Pearse, are you ready to proceed?"

"Yes, my lord."

A jailer escorted the very pregnant defendant from a side room to the dock. Her hair was undone and she appeared not to have slept in days.

"Anna Perenna, you have been brought before this court to stand trial for the capital charge of willful murder. Do you understand the charge?"

The widow stared straight ahead, unresponsive

"Excuse me, my lord," said a gentleman rising from his seat near the front of the court. "I am Charles Stinson and I represent the defendant in this matter. She has spoken nothing of this case to us. In fact, she has spoken not a word since she was taken into custody a week Friday last—not to us, not to anyone, as far as we can establish. She cannot understand the charge. She is therefore not fit to stand trial."

"Mr. Pearse," asked the judge, "what have you to say on this matter?"

Pearse rose. "My lord, we will establish, through undisputed testimony, that the prisoner absolutely understood her actions on the very day of the murder. We will provide witnesses immediately, if you so desire, who will testify that she has, every day since the shooting, consistently obeyed the instructions and followed the commands given to her. She clearly understands her jailers and matrons. Admittedly her demeanor and behavior have been docile, but that is common of prisoners who feel the ache of culpability for their deeds. Except for her refusal to speak, no one, not even my colleague Mr. Stinson, can point to a single iota of evidence suggesting this woman is not fit to stand trial for her crime. If we are to not try a prisoner simply because he refuses to speak, then there will be no more trials. Why would any prisoner choose to speak and thereby put himself at risk?"

Prompted for his response, Stinson said, "If she does not speak before this court, my lord, she can not defend herself. If she will not speak to us, then we cannot defend her."

"Every prisoner has a right to silence," said the judge.

"If she voluntarily chooses not to speak, my lord, then yes," Stinson argued. "But if a defendant is incapable of forming the thoughts necessary for speech, then this court has no right to prosecute her."

"Do you have any evidence that she is incapable of forming thoughts on the matter?"

Stinson hemmed and hawed before answering, "No, my lord."

"Then we shall proceed. Anna Perenna, how do you plead, guilty or not guilty?"

Anna stood silent in the dock, her gaze indeterminate.

"In lieu of a response, this court enters a plea of not guilty for the prisoner."

"Then, my lord, we enter a plea of *non compos mentis*," said Mr. Stinson, still standing in the gallery.

"That is not a plea, that is a defense, one which you bear the burden to prove."

"Very good, my lord," Stinson said, unabashed.

The prosecutor rose to proceed at Judge Blair's leave. He hooked his thumbs in the lower pockets of his vest and nodded to the jurymen.

"Gentlemen," he began, "this trial will be of no great difficulty for me to present, and no great difficulty for you to decide. Just ten days ago, on the morning of the thirteenth of March, the prisoner raised a loaded pistol to her husband and put a bullet through the center of his forehead. No one will dispute that simple, all-important fact. Not even Mr. Stinson will dispute it. Instead, he will tell you that she was mad when she shot him. Not angry because he threatened to leave her, which he certainly would have been justified in doing, given her delicate state resulting from her indelicate behavior during his long absence. No, not that sort of mad. He will argue that she was mad in the medical sense of not being sane, and therefore not legally liable for firing a bullet through her husband's head. Mr. Stinson will argue that she was not so mad that she was screaming and thrashing about, or cowering in a corner, nor otherwise without control of her physical faculties, for if she were, she'd have been unable to willfully land a bullet directly in the center of her husband's forehead with her first and only shot. He will agree that she was capable of doing that, yet he will allege that she is somehow not responsible for such a careful, accurate shot, not responsible for such a deliberate, well-executed, cold-blooded killing."

He paused and smiled grimly as the jurymen nodded agreement.

"I call as my first witness," he said, turning back to the courtroom, "Constable Henry Murger."

The hulking uniformed policeman who had directed the removal of John Hawkins and David Lindsey from the crime scene filled the witness box. He raised his right hand for the oath, standing proud and erect, seemingly ready for any question that might be put to him.

"Constable Murger," said Mr. Pearse, after the swearing in, "you arrived at 22 Torquay Terrace quite soon after the shooting took place."

"Yes, sir. I did."

"Please describe to the jury what you found upon entering the house."

"Certainly," said the constable. "I noticed first two small men wrestling on the floor. Neither seemed in danger of hurting the other. In fact, neither seemed a risk to anyone but his own self. I noticed next, to my left, the body of a tall man slipped to the floor, blood streaking down the wall leading behind his head, and a large bullet wound in his forehead, one of the largest I have seen in my career. From my right, I heard a woman blubbering, wailing for forgiveness over and over again. Turning my attention in that direction, sir, I then noticed two women on a couch, the aggrieved being held by the other. I saw all this in an instant, then I broke up the squabble on the floor, lifting each man by his collar and had them placed in the Maria."

"The Maria?" the prosecutor innocently cut in.

"The Black Maria, sir. It's what we call our prisoner's wagon."

"I see. Thank you. Now did you notice anything else?"

"The woman who wasn't crying for mercy, she informed me that a pistol had been kicked under the couch during the men's scuffle. I had one of my constables recover it and hand it to me. On my examination, it revealed itself to be a Colt 1851 Navy revolving holster pistol, thirty-six caliber. I examined the chambers. Five contained cartridges. One was empty. By sight, touch, and smell I could tell that one cartridge had just been fired from that chamber. I examined the blood splashed on the wall, and, as expected, found a bullet hole near the center of it. I concluded that someone had fired the revolver, shooting the victim in the forehead, after which the bullet exited the back of the victim's head and embedded itself in the wall. I then determined to await the arrival of the detectives, to allow them to extract the bullet from the wall and conduct the interviews.

"It sounds as if you should be a detective yourself, Constable," Pearse said with a crooning solicitousness.

"No thank you, sir," Murger replied, much to the amusement of the judge, jury, and audience.

When the chuckles died out, Pearse spread his hands in invitation. "Please continue, Constable."

"I awaited the coroner to examine and remove the body. I had several of my men take statements from the crowd gathering outdoors, and from the neighbors. Some had heard a single gunshot; others had gathered for the spectacle. You'll often have that, lookers-on. Some familiar with the household advised that the victim was Lt. William Perenna, an officer in Her Majesty's Army, recently home from a lengthy tour in Afghanistan. The neighbors also noted that his wife, Anna Perenna, was many months with child, and they speculated that infidelity led to the murder of the wronged party."

"Objection," said Mr. Stinson, rising to his feet.

"Sustained," said the judge. "Constable Murger, please stick to the facts."

"Yes, my lord. My apologies, my lord."

"Constable," continued the prosecutor, "was the prisoner the woman whom you witnessed in tears, at the home on Torquay Terrace, begging forgiveness?"

"Yes, sir."

"Did she seem sad to you?"

"She certainly did, sir."

"As if she had recently committed some great sin for which she knew she must atone?"

"Absolutely, sir."

"Did she seem mad?"

"Sir?"

"Was she ranting? Was she apparently in the grip of a violent brain fever? Or perhaps huddled in a corner, sucking her thumb?"

"No sir, nothing like that," said the constable, matter-of-factly.

"She was just terribly sad and crying out for absolution?"

"Yes, sir. That is all."

"Thank you, Constable. I have no further questions for this witness, my lord."

"Mr. Stinson, do you have any questions for the witness?"

"Yes, my lord. Just a few," said the barrister, rising and approaching.

"You are a constable for the Bristol Police, is that correct?"

"Since the spring of eighteen hundred and sixty-eight, sir. Going on my eleventh year."

Stinson hummed appreciatively. "Admirable. Yet you have no desire to be a detective with the Bristol Police."

"No, sir, I do not."

"I assume you have no desire, either, to be a doctor, or, more specifically, an alienist."

"You are correct, sir."

"Given all your experience as a constable rather than as an alienist, do you feel qualified to determine the prisoner's state of mind at the very instant she pulled the trigger?"

The constable pondered the question before answering, "The very instant, sir? I was not in the room when she pulled the trigger."

"So, do you know what was in her mind the very instant she pulled the trigger?"

"Ah, no, I do not," he answered, adding, as an afterthought, "sir."

"Thank you, Constable. I have no further questions, my lord."

"Call your next witness, Mr. Pearse," the judge said as he inspected a splotch of what was apparently a previous day's lunch on his robes.

"The prosecution calls Dr. Daniel Weston."

The tall gentleman, clean shaven and fastidiously dressed, rose from the crowd and stepped into the witness box, where he raised his right hand and swore that he would tell the truth.

"Dr. Weston, did you perform the necropsy on the body of Lt. William Perenna?"

"I did perform an autopsy on the body of a person presented to me as Lt. William Perenna, yes."

"I presume, Doctor, that you are merely being precise and cautious in your answers. You have no reason to believe that the body was that of someone *other* than Lt. William Perenna, is that correct?"

"You are correct, sir. I have no reason to presume otherwise."

"Did you determine a cause of death?"

"I did."

When Pearse realized that no exposition to his question was coming, he pressed on. "Dr. Weston, what was your determination?"

"A gunshot wound to the head, the bullet entering at the forehead, approximately three inches below the top of the head, and exiting almost directly behind."

"I presume death was instantaneous?"

"The victim undoubtedly died within moments of the bullet passing through his brain."

"From your examination of the body, could you approximate the diameter of the bullet that killed Lt. Perenna?"

"Yes."

"If I were to inform you that a thirty-six caliber bullet was recovered from the wall directly behind Lt. Perenna's head, at least where his head had been, just prior to the shooting, would that be consistent with your approximation of the bullet's diameter?"

"It would be consistent," said the doctor.

"If I were to inform you that a thirty-six caliber revolver had been found at the feet of the prisoner, would that be consistent with your approximation of the bullet's diameter?"

"It would be consistent," Dr. Weston repeated.

"I have no more questions for this witness, my lord."

"Mr. Stinson," asked Judge Blair, "have you any questions for Dr. Weston?"

"I do, my lord."

"Please be prompt, then."

"Certainly, my lord. Dr. Weston, did you examine the entirety of Lt. Perenna's body?"

"I conducted a thorough external examination of the deceased's body. I did not open it to perform an internal examination, since the coroner did not request that I do so, the cause of death being immediately evident."

"Did you prepare a written report of your examination?"

"I did."

"I presume that is the report in your hand?"

"It is."

"Would you please read what you recorded regarding the genitals of Lt. Perenna?"

A sudden raucous explosion of shouts and hoots went up from the audience.

The prosecutor was quick to his feet, shouting to be heard above the din, "Objection! Such evidence is absolutely immaterial in this case."

Judge Blair shouted the courtroom to order.

"It is quite material, my lord," said Stinson calmly. "You took care to remind me that the defense bears the burden of proving *non compos mentis*, and Dr. Weston's findings are of utmost relevance to that issue."

"You may proceed, Mr. Stinson," said the judge, "but I caution you to do so with all due discretion."

"I shall, my lord. Now, Doctor, would you please read what you wrote regarding the genitals of Lt. Perenna?"

The doctor donned his gold-framed pince-nez and, in a reedy voice, recited from his report. "The external genitalia are remarkable for a single, firm ulceration on the penis. The ulceration is oval shaped, one and three quarters inch long and one quarter inch wide. The ulceration has the clean base and sharp borders of a chancre."

A woman in the audience swooned. A constable escorted her from the courtroom and, to fill the seat, admitted an excited man from the crowd outside.

"Dr. Weston, would you please explain to the jurymen what a chancre is?"

From their pained countenances, it seemed clear that most of the jurymen already knew what a chancre was, and what it represented.

"A chancre is an ulceration, an open sore, that appears on the body, usually, on a male at least, on the external genitalia, during the first stage of syphilis."

Murmurs flowed through the audience.

"So, Doctor, do you believe that Lt. Perenna was suffering from syphilis when he was shot?"

"I suspect that he was, yes."

"Given that he had contracted the disease, by what means would that have come about?"

The doctor was impassive. "Through intimate relations with another, already afflicted."

"And if he would later have had intimate relations with a third party, would she have contracted the disease herself?"

"At that stage of the infection, almost certainly, yes."

"And if that third party, that woman, was pregnant, could her child have been subsequently afflicted?"

"Yes indeed," the doctor said.

Stinson, struck a pose of reflection, then walked a small circle before returning to his questioning.

"Dr. Weston, are you familiar with the term *brain fever*?"

"I am."

"Would you describe it for the jurymen, please."

"Certainly. Brain fever is an inflammation of the brain, attended with acute fever and delirium. The term is descriptive of symptoms rather than of cause. Various pathogens can cause inflammation of the brain. *Mycobacterium tuberculosis*, for example, sometimes finds its way to the meninges, inflaming those tissues and causing cerebral meningitis. That would be just one form of brain fever."

"And what of popular usage? Have you heard the term

used to describe any delirium or frenzy, even one not caused by an inflammation?"

"Yes," said the doctor, appearing displeased with the non-clinical application of the term.

"Would a person under the grip of brain fever be capable of controlling his or her actions?"

"Assuming the person was indeed suffering delirium or frenzy, then, by definition, that person would be unable to control his or her actions."

"So some suffer delirium or frenzy brought on by factors other than inflammation?"

"Yes."

"What would some of those factors be?"

"Excluding inflammation, I assume some of those afflictions have a psychological basis."

"Do you know of women who presented with deranged behavior as a result of encountering something shocking, disturbing, repulsive, or the like?"

"Yes, women seem susceptible to that sort of disturbance."

"Allow me to present you with a hypothetical before I ask my next question. Please presume, for the purpose of my next question, a wife long separated from her husband, an army lieutenant serving in a foreign country. Presume that the woman has been unfaithful in her husband's absence, and has become encumbered with child. Presume that, upon the husband's return, the woman suffers not only the shame of her infidelity, but also the horror of her husband's syphilitic affliction, the fear for her own safety and that of her unborn child. Given that hypothetical situation, Doctor, do you believe it possible that the woman could suffer a fit of brain fever?"

Following a lengthy pause, Dr. Weston said, "It is possible."

"I have no more questions for this witness, my lord."

"I do!" said the prosecutor, rising. "Dr. Weston, in the exceptionally unlikely event that any woman would suffer brain fever under the silly hypothetical put to you by the desperate Mr. Stinson—"

"Objection!" interrupted the desperate Mr. Stinson. "I object to the mischaracterization of my hypothetical, and to the misrepresentation of the state of the defense's case. It is patently clear, my lord, that the learned prosecutor is more concerned for the state of his own case, and it should be beneath him to respond in such irresponsible, odious fashion."

"Sit, Mr. Stinson," said the judge. "Rephrase, Mr. Pearse. And behave, the both of you. We have no time for such delays to these proceedings. We are moving along much too slowly as it is."

"My apologies, my lord," said Pearse, bowing slightly to the bench. "Doctor, when a person experiences brain fever, whether of medical or mysterious origin, do they spontaneously recover within minutes of its onset?"

"In my experience, psychological attacks of brain fever are almost always prolonged, lasting days, sometimes weeks, sometimes for the life of the patient."

Pearse looked like that cat that swallowed the canary. "So, if someone experienced brain fever as the result of an argument, say, and she committed a heinous crime immediately after the fever's onset, that person would not spontaneously recover from the affliction within the next minute."

"No, not likely."

"One final question. Assuming someone was suffering brain fever, and therefore unable to control herself, would she be able to put a bullet dead in the center of the forehead of a man standing across the room, first shot, only shot?"

"It seems exceptionally unlikely."

"Thank you, Doctor. I have no more questions of this witness, my lord."

Judge Blair, stifling a yawn, said, "You may step down, Doctor. Call your next witness, Mr. Pearse."

Pearse announced, "The prosecution calls Miss Louise Hawkins."

chapter fourteen
THE TESTIMONY

As Louise rose from the audience and limped to the witness box, those in the courtroom who had not already gawked at her were shocked by her appearance. She looked to have been thoroughly thrashed by someone who disliked her intensely. Her nose appeared to be broken, her empurpled eyes painfully swollen, and those able to perceive anything other than her facial injuries further observed the bandage on her left hand and the cane in her right. All these impairments were at serious odds with her serene expression and forthright manner.

In the witness box, she stood unsteadily on her good foot as she leaned the cane against the railing to raise her bandaged hand for the oath.

"Do you swear that the evidence which you shall give at this trial of Anna Perenna for the murder of William Perenna shall be the truth, the whole truth, and nothing but the truth, so help you God?" asked the clerk.

"I do," she answered.

"Miss Hawkins," Judge Blair asked, "might we get you a chair?"

"I will stand, my lord," said Louise, regaining her cane.

"I pray that these injuries are in no way related to this case."

"My injuries are of my own making, my lord. They are the natural result of my own carelessness and lack of preparation."

"Very well. You may proceed, Mr. Pearse."

"I won't keep you long, Miss Hawkins," said the prosecutor, smiling. "As I understand it, you were the first person to enter 22 Torquay Terrace after the shooting there, a week ago Thursday last, is that correct?"

Louise turned to the jurymen to answer, "As far as I know, I was the first person to enter the house in question, following the shooting. And yes, the shooting of which I speak took place on thirteen March, the Thursday one week ago last."

She turned back to the prosecutor, who showed mild puzzlement at her behavior, but continued. "What prompted you to enter the house?"

Again, Louise turned to the jurymen before answering, "I heard a gunshot. I wanted to assist however I might."

She turned back to the prosecutor. He chuckled.

"It seems odd that you address the jurors, Miss Hawkins. It is I who ask the questions."

In the absence of a question, she kept her silence. Pearse fidgeted with his pocket watch, having sudden misgivings about this woman he had called to the witness box.

He asked, "Why do you address them so?"

She turned to the jurors.

"I address you directly, sirs, since you are the jurymen in this case. As such, you and you alone are to adduce the facts in this case. Not even the honorable judge of this court may instruct you, advise you, or suggest to you how you might consider the facts. I answer directly to you, gentlemen, since you will decide on the truthfulness of what I shall testify to under my oath."

She turned back to face the prosecutor.

"It is unusual," he said. "That is all. That and it seems a bit rude for a woman to turn away from a gentleman asking questions of her."

Louise awaited his question.

"You are, after all, my witness."

Louise continued her impassive vigil.

"Are you not?" Pearse asked.

"No, sir, I am not," she said evenly, addressing him directly. "I am no person's witness other than my own."

"Please get on with it, Mr. Pearse," said the judge.

"Certainly, my lord," said the prosecutor, with another nod to the bench. To Louise he asked, "Where were you when you heard the gunshot?"

She turned to the jurors before answering, as she had determined to do for her entire testimony.

"I was walking along Torquay Terrace, six house fronts away."

"Do you live there?"

"I do not," she answered.

"When you heard the shot, you did not run away, as is the natural inclination."

As there was no question, Louise did not speak.

"Is that correct?" appended Mr. Pearse with growing agitation.

"Mr. Pearse is correct in that I did not run away," Louise told the jurymen. "I cannot, however, speak to the natural inclination of others, only mine. Apparently it is not *my* natural inclination to run from a gunshot. It was my first such experience, so I have no other evidence on which to base my answer."

One of the jurymen nodded at her, offering the smallest hint of a smile from beneath his mustache.

"And as I understand it," continued Pearce, "you injured your ankle as you ran to the house." After a momentary silence, he added, "Is that correct?"

"That is correct," Louise said to the jury. "I twisted my ankle on a cobblestone."

"That must have been painful. It has been a week and four days since, and still you bandage your ankle and make use of a cane." Someone coughed from the gallery. Pearse sighed. "I realize that you do not wish to be here, Miss Hawkins. I assure you that none of us are gladdened by these circumstances."

"Objection!" said Stinson, taking to his feet. "It is the prosecutor's obligation to ask questions of this witness, my lord. Instead he lectures."

"Pray forgive me, my lord," said Pearse, preempting Judge Blair's reprimand. "Miss Hawkins, what did you see when you entered the house where the shooting had just taken place?"

To the jury, Louise said, "Directly in front of the door, approximately in the center of the front room, I saw a woman standing. Sidelong, I perceived she was with child, quite far along, and was asking repeatedly for forgiveness, though she never made clear any sin that might have prompted her requests. My attention was drawn, almost immediately, to the object of her fixed gaze. It was a horrible splash of blood and brain matter on the wall, flowing downward to the body of a tall man in military dress. He was nearly on his back. Only his head still touched the wall, directly beneath the bloody streaks. Even as I looked on, blood from the back of his head continued to pool on the floor. Between his feet and hers, a revolver lay on the ground."

"It must have been terrible for you," Pearse said. "That woman you saw in the center of the room, begging to be forgiven, was she the one now standing in the dock, the one identified to this court as Anna Perenna?"

Louise looked at Anna, who was seemingly catatonic.

"The woman in the dock," said Louise, "is the woman I saw in the center of that room." She continued studying Anna until interrupted by Pearse's next question.

"You say that the pistol lay between the victim and the shooter. Would it not be more accurate to describe it as being at the feet of Anna Perenna?"

Louise looked at the lawyer, Stinson. Surely, she thought, he would object, this time, to the characterization of his client as the shooter. Stinson, however, merely scribbled notes on a sheet of paper and did not meet her eye. She therefore turned to the jury and answered, simply, "No."

"No?" asked a surprised Pearse. "But the scene you just described—"

She spun on the prosecutor and said, "You summon me here, sir, and you put me under oath. You then ask me a question expecting one answer, and challenge me when I give another. As I have testified, I was the first person in that room, as far as I know. I do know with certainty that you were not there when I spied the pistol on the floor, yet somehow you claim to better know the position of it. Perhaps, sir, you should stand here in the box and answer your own questions."

The audience and jurymen smiled and poked one another.

"Miss Hawkins," the judge said, "You will answer the questions as they are put to you. Mr. Pearse, you will be more precise and less accusatory with your questions. She is, after all, your witness. Or so you claim."

"Very good, my lord," said the prosecutor with a bow. "Miss Hawkins, in your estimation, how far was the pistol from Anna Perenna's feet?"

"The pistol was approximately four feet from her," she answered to the jurymen.

"But it was certainly closer to the prisoner than it was to the victim. Is that not so?"

"The distance from Anna Perenna to the wall was approximately eleven feet. Lt. Perenna stood six feet tall. Given that his entire body, save his head, rested on the floor, his feet lay approximately five feet from the wall. Simple mathematics tells you that the pistol was only two feet from Lt. Perenna's feet, closer to him than to the defendant."

"However, from where he stood when she shot him, the pistol must have been much closer to her than to him. Is that correct?"

Louise took time formulating her answer, hoping that Mr. Stinson would object before an answer would be demanded of her, but he merely observed the proceedings, doe-eyed. An unorthodox thought sprang into her head.

She addressed Judge Blair. "Objection! The prosecutor presumes facts not in evidence, my lord, namely that the defendant shot Lt. Perenna, and that Lt. Perenna was standing near the wall when he was shot."

"Objection!" stammered the prosecutor. "Instruct the witness that she is not allowed to object."

"Mr. Pearse," said the judge with gravity, "you forget yourself at your peril. Do not instruct this court on how it shall handle this or any other witness. You may object, as you have, and you may state the grounds for your objection, but you shall not again demand that this court bow to your objections."

"My sincere apology to the court, my lord," said the prosecutor, visibly rattled, with an uneasy mixture of contrition and frustration.

"Now for you, Miss Hawkins," said Judge Blair, somewhat less firmly. "You are not to object to the questions put to you. If there is an objection to be made, Mr. Stinson will make it." He turned to the defense attorney. "Do you wish to object to Mr. Pearse's last question?"

Stinson rose with plain reluctance. He responded halfheartedly. "Yes, my lord. I object to the last question as presuming facts not in evidence."

"More specifically, Mr. Pearse," sighed the judge.

"He presumes my client shot Lt. Perenna, though no evidence has yet been brought to bear that she was the shooter. He presumes the victim stood against the wall, though no evidence has been introduced on the matter of where he was standing when shot."

"May I respond, my lord?" asked the prosecutor. "I concede the latter point, and I will not again treat it as fact unless I first bring evidence to establish it as such. With respect to the prisoner being the shooter, however, I suggest that the issue has been well established. My colleague argues *non compos mentis* as the defense in this case. He thereby stipulates that his client *did* shoot her husband but bears no responsibility because she was not of competent mind at the time. He cannot offer a convoluted, contradictory defense that Mrs. Perenna did not shoot her husband but was incompetent if she did."

"You are correct, Mr. Pearse. There is no question before this court as to who shot Lt. William Perenna. It is accepted as fact that the prisoner did. The only question, as per the defense's choosing, is whether the prisoner was mentally competent when she shot her husband. Therefore, with respect to the issue of the prisoner being the shooter, I overrule Mr. Stinson's objection. With respect to the victim's location when he was shot, I sustain it. Rephrase your question, Mr. Pearse."

"Yes, my lord. Thank you, my lord," Pearse kowtowed.

"And do move this along more briskly," the judge added. "We have another case yet to hear, jury deliberations to await, and justice to be meted out."

Thanking the judge once more, Pearse turned back to his witness. He strove to retrieve his previous train of thought.

"Uh, oh, yes, Miss Hawkins, assuming Lt. Perenna was standing near the wall when his wife, the defendant, shot him in the head, would not the pistol, once it fell from her hand, have been much closer to her than to the victim, at least before he slid to the floor?"

The room waited anxiously for the next twist, which Louise supplied by turning to the judge, saying, "I cannot answer him, my lord."

With increasing impatience, Judge Blair said, "You shall answer the question put to you."

"I cannot, my lord."

"Pray, why not?"

"Because you had me take an oath, in our Lord's name no less, that I would tell the truth, the whole truth, and nothing but the truth. I cannot observe that oath and answer the question as it has been put to me."

"And why is that?" asked the judge as he leaned forward, imposing his substantial girth on her field of vision.

"He instructs me to base my answer to his question on the presumption that Lt. Perenna was standing near the wall when Anna Perenna shot him."

"He formulated his question as a hypothetical, Miss Hawkins, not as a statement of fact. That is allowed."

"Why does he insist, my lord, that I answer his hypothetical?" Louise begged. "I have already testified clearly, and as accurately as I am capable, regarding the distances involved."

"It is his prerogative, though now I too begin to wonder about the thrust of his questioning." The judge turned his attention to the prosecutor. "Why, Mr. Pearse, are you insistent about putting the pistol at the foot of the prisoner?"

"It is merely more evidence of her guilt, my lord," Pearse said. "She dropped the pistol after she shot him, and it landed at her feet. It is that simple, but suddenly it has become unduly complicated. I fear this witness would rather find herself in contempt of court than follow your instructions to answer my questions."

"Mr. Pearse," said the judge, "does the position of the weapon on the floor have anything to do with establishing the prisoner was or was not *non compos mentis* when she shot the victim?"

"No, my lord. Not in any fashion that I can conceive."

"Then why are you asking it? Have I not made amply clear that her sanity is the only issue to be pursued here?"

"Yes, my lord. I understand. I withdraw the question."

"Very good. You may continue your questioning. And again, Miss Hawkins, you shall answer the questions as they are put to you. This trial shall continue apace, else I shall impose sanctions."

"Please, my lord," Louise said, fixing the judge with her earnest blue-green eyes. "I learned from the coroner, one Mr. Quinton Welch, that the jurors are to be supreme in matters of fact, that the judge is not to even advise them, much less instruct them, as to the facts. Mr. Welch was quite clear on that point, and I trust him on this matter, since, as he twice took pains to inform us, he has yet to have any of his findings quashed. Even you, my lord, did not correct me when, in one of my early answers, I explained to the jurymen that they, and only they, are responsible for determining the facts of the case. Yet you take the most fundamental of all facts from them! You tell them that they are not to decide whether the victim died at the hands of the defendant or at those of another. You go so far as to forbid these gentlemen from asking any question that might establish whether or not she shot her husband at all."

Reporters scribbled furiously, and before Judge Blair could fully chew and swallow what Louise had just served him, she continued apace.

"It is to this misappropriation of the jurors' responsibility that I object. I object not in a legal sense, in the name of Her Majesty the Queen, since you forbid me that, but instead in common parlance, in the name of the common people for whom this court claims to seek justice."

Judge Blair sank back, pondering his next move.

"I cannot enforce my view under the color of authority as you can," she continued, "or under threat of swift and certain punishment, but I can choose to not answer questions improperly put to me. And, having sworn an oath to this court and to God, I do refuse to answer such questions, even under pain of poverty or punishment."

From the witness box, Louise turned her head to gaze at the prisoner in the dock, who, for the first time, looked back.

"This court will be in recess for one quarter hour," Judge Blair intoned, heaving his mass erect. "Mr. Pearse, Mr. Stinson, I will see you both in my chamber."

Anna Perenna was escorted from the dock. Louise spent the entire recess standing in the witness box, leaning heavily on her cane, trying unsuccessfully to relieve her increasingly painful ankle. When the judge and lawyers returned from chamber, they all looked surprised to see her still there. Before settling behind his lofty bench, the judge addressed her.

"Miss Hawkins, there was no need for you to stand during the recess."

"I stand by my own choosing, my lord."

"Would you care now for a chair?" he inquired.

"Very kind of you, my lord. I choose to stand."

"As you like," he said. As he took his seat, everyone in the courtroom took theirs. "Bring in the prisoner."

Anna Perenna entered, still chained, but with her head now fully upright. Upon gaining her position in the dock, she turned to regard Louise, whose bruised stare met her own with equal resolve. Anna's composure seemed disturbed by the direction of Louise's answers, and where they might lead.

"We will proceed as follows," began the judge in a most decisive voice, turning first to the jury. "The prosecution and the defense shall inquire into both the circumstances of Lt. Perenna's death and the state of the prisoner's mind at the time of the shooting. After all the evidence has been compiled by this questioning and testimony, and after I have explained the laws relating to the crime charged hereby, I will pass this case to you. You will compare the facts of the case, as you determine them to be facts, against the law as I will explain it to you. You will first decide whether the prosecution has proven to you, beyond a reasonable doubt, that Lt. Perenna died at the hands of the prisoner. If you so find, then and only then will you decide whether the defense has proven to you, to a moral certainty, that the prisoner was not responsible for her actions because she was *non compos mentis*, not of sound mind."

Judge Blair then addressed the prosecutor.

"You, Mr. Pearse, will prosecute this case aggressively, but you shall do so properly. You may ask difficult questions, but you shall not ask unfair ones. You shall not presume to answer for any witness by the form of your question. For the record, acknowledge now that you understand these instructions."

"I understand, my lord," said the prosecutor, popping up only as long as it took to respond.

"You, Mr. Stinson, shall defend your client aggressively, both with respect to the circumstances of the crime and to your client's state of mind at the time of the shooting. For the record, acknowledge now that you understand these instructions."

"I understand the instructions of this court, my lord," the defense piped, then sat as quickly as had his colleague.

"And you, Miss Hawkins," the judge said, turning to her. "You shall answers the questions as they are fairly put to you. You shall not object to them, lest I find you in contempt. For the record, please now acknowledge your understanding of my instructions."

"I understand you completely, my lord," Louise said with a slight nod, which plainly relieved Judge Blair a great deal.

"Mr. Pearse, you may continue your questioning. Miss Hawkins, I remind you that you are still under oath."

"Of that, my lord, you can be assured," she said.

Addressing Louise, the prosecutor asked, "Who did you notice to be in the room when you first entered?"

"I saw first the defendant, whom I now understand to be Anna Perenna," Louise explained to the jury. "I noticed next the body of the victim, whom I now understand to have been Lt. Perenna."

"You noticed no one else in the room," observed the prosecutor. Louise's lack of reply sent him into a momentary fit, chewing the inside of his cheek as if it might prevent him from shouting. He soon stopped his jaws working and sheepishly excused himself to the court, realizing the form of his previous remark. He appended, "Did you notice anyone else in the room?"

"Other than one soon to be born," she said to the jury, winning numerous chuckles from around the room, "I noticed no one else in the room."

"Did you see anyone running from the room?"

"No."

"Did you see any evidence of someone else having been recently in the room?"

"No," she replied.

"Did you see any evidence that someone had shot Lt. Perenna from outside the room?"

"No, I did not."

"Did you see any gun other than the pistol on the floor?" Pearse asked, eyes to the ceiling as though reciting a litany.

"No, sir.

"Was the pistol close enough to Anna Perenna that it could have landed there, had she dropped it?"

"Yes."

"Did you hear Anna Perenna repeatedly asking for forgiveness?"

"I did."

"Then, Miss Hawkins, have you any doubt that the prisoner, Anna Perenna, was the person who shot her husband, Lt. William Perenna?"

Turning to the jury, Louise paused for effect before answering, "Yes, I doubt it. In fact, I am certain that she did not."

chapter fifteen
CONTEMPT AND REVELATION

The audience erupted in hubbub. Reporters shouted questions over one another. The judge, in turn, shouted them to order, on pain of eviction, to imperfect result.

Anna Perenna showed no positive reaction to the faith Louise professed in her innocence. Indeed, she uncomprehendingly looked out over the jury, her distress growing more evident with the turn of events.

"Chief Constable," said the judge, pointing to a reporter who had failed to quiet himself, "remove that man from the courtroom."

Louise saw Anna put a hand gently to her swollen belly, as if to soothe the child within. Most everyone else craned to observe two constables dragging the unruly reporter from the room, pencil and pad in hand, scribbling even as he was being dragged down the aisle.

"Place him in the wagon for the duration of the trial," shouted the judge.

The reporters and their readers quieted quickly then. Anna caressed her midriff, as the world seemed to swirl around them.

"You will explain yourself, Miss Hawkins," said Judge Blair, jowls quivering.

Louise turned from Anna. "Yes, my lord." To the jury she said, "The defendant could not have shot the lieutenant from afar, as doing so would have left a circular hole in his—"

"To me, Miss Hawkins," said the judge. "You will explain yourself to me. Do I make myself clear?"

"—forehead," she continued ignoring Judge Blair's order. "I saw his wound when I was in the room. It could only have been a contact wound, that is, the muzzle was in direct contact with the flesh when the revolver was fired."

"Objection!" shouted the prosecutor. "She is not qualified in forensic medicine."

"Sustained," said the judge. "Miss Hawkins, you shall not testify to that which you cannot know."

"Nor could the defendant have been the one who put the muzzle to Lt. Perenna's forehead," Louise went on, her voice rising against the court's efforts to silence her. "She is much too short. It is a simple matter of angles, as any of you who play billiards will understand. Had Anna Perenna shot him, the bullet would have been found higher on the wall, not at the same level as the hole in his forehead."

With that, she fell silent and gently bowed her head to the enraged Judge Blair.

"Miss Hawkins, I find you in contempt of this court, and I impose a fine upon you of twenty shillings. If you should again ignore the instructions of this court, I shan't hesitate to impose an additional fine of forty shillings. Do I make myself clear?"

"Yes, my lord," she nodded in earnest.

Judge Blair calmed. "These fantastical claims that you make," he asked, after mopping his brow, "have you any scholarly work with which to back them up, or are they merely fantasies of your own devising?"

"No, my lord," she said.

"One or the other, Miss Hawkins. Which is it? Can you cite any work by scholars to support your claims, or not?"

"I cannot, my lord."

"Then these are merely ideas plucked from thin air?" he pressed.

"They are neither fantasies, nor am I alone in holding them as fact. My conclusions are well-founded upon the autopsy report, made public at the inquest, upon the condition of the body, which I had the misfortune to observe, and upon experiments, to which I have been party."

"I see. Well, it is therefore the decision of this court," he said, "that since you are neither qualified in forensic medicine nor possessing scholarly work to support your claims, you shall not presume to testify regarding matters of forensic medicine. Mr. Pearse, do you have a witness who can shine more light upon these issues?"

The prosecutor looked to his left and right, as if another witness was at hand. "Not at the moment, my lord. Er, uh, I could recall the surgeon."

"You shall, sir, and we shall learn of these matters properly. Constable, I instruct you to locate Dr. Weston and return him promptly to this courtroom. Mr. Pearse, you shall continue with your questioning of this witness, focusing now on the prisoner's claim of *non compos mentis.*"

"Yes, my lord. One moment, please, to collect my thoughts," the prosecutor said, nervously smoothing his vest.

"I advise you to collect them carefully, Mr. Pearse," cautioned the judge. After Pearse had paced and muttered awhile in feverish thought, Judge Blair prodded him. "Whenever you are ready, Mr. Pearse."

"Yes, my lord, ah, erm, I believe that, uh—"

"Do get on with it, Mr. Pearse."

"I have no further questions of this witness, my lord," he said, and quickly sat.

"Very good. She is now your witness, Mr. Stinson."

"Thank you, my lord," he said, rising from his chair. "Miss Hawkins, you were the first witness on the scene, is that correct?"

"As far as I know," Louise answered to the jury, "I was the first person, after the shooting, to enter the Perennas' home."

"And as the first, therefore, to witness my client's behavior immediately after the shooting, please tell us, did she seem addled?"

"Presuming, that Mr. Stinson uses *addled* in the sense of being unable to think clearly," Louise told the jury, "I do not know if Anna Perenna was addled when I entered the room."

"Allow me to phrase my question differently. When you first observed my client's behavior, was it that of a normal person?"

"I do not know with any certainty how a normal person might behave when—"

"Was she not repeating the same phrase, again and again, as one in great mental shock would be expected to?"

Louise, still speaking to the jurymen, answered, "She did repeatedly say 'forgive me' or 'God, forgive me,' or some variation of that phrase. She said nothing else while I was there."

"In your experience, is that the behavior of a woman in command of her mental faculties?"

"As I have already endeavored to explain, I do not know how a woman might normally behave in such abnormal circumstances."

"Did she take any notice of you when you entered the house?" asked Stinson.

"No."

"Other than weeping and crying out, did she do anything?"

"She did not."

"You attempted to solace her, you told us earlier, by sitting with her on the couch, is that correct?"

"It is," said Louise.

"Did you find that she was somewhat stiff, rigid in her movements, a bit mechanical?"

"She was."

"As I understand it, your efforts were to little avail, save for limiting her anguished refrain. Correct?"

"Yes, she seemed beyond comforting, but she did stop asking for forgiveness at some point."

"Are you aware that she has not spoken a word since?" asked Stinson, casting a short look at his client in the dock.

"That is my understanding from my reading of newspapers. I certainly have not been with her at every moment since."

"Are you aware that she continues to stare blankly ahead of herself?"

"That, too, is my understanding, though I have seen her look about, on occasion, to take in these environs and proceedings."

"But in the main, she stares forward even here, is that correct?"

"As far as I am aware."

"Are you aware that she does not feed herself, take drink, or tend to herself, but requires aid in all basic functions of the day-to-day?"

"I understand that to be so," Louise said.

Apparently satisfied, he moved to another line of questioning. "You are aware of the autopsy report, are you not?"

"I am well aware of it."

"And you have heard the testimony in this courtroom regarding that report, have you not?"

"I have."

"And you are therefore aware that Lt. Perenna was syphilitic, correct?"

"Yes, I am aware of that fact."

"Do you understand that Lt. Perenna could have passed that insidious affliction to his wife and, through her, to their unborn child?"

"I do understand that, yes."

"If you were in Anna Perenna's difficult situation, having just learned that your husband may have placed you and your child at grave risk, might that drive you mad?"

"Objection!" shouted the prosecutor. "The witness is no more qualified to answer such a question than to discuss forensic medicine."

"Sustained. You will not answer, Miss Hawkins," Judge Blair instructed.

"Is that not what drove her insane, Miss Hawkins?" Stinson persisted over the judge's orders. "Was that not what overshadowed her mind just before she shot him?"

"You are out of order, Mr. Stinson, and you shall pursue such questioning no further," the judge thundered. "One more question of that nature, and I shall find you in contempt."

Regardless, Louise turned to the jurymen, saying, over the judge's admonitions, "She is a mystery to me, this Anna Perenna. I cannot read the contents of her mind. I cannot find insanity there, as Mr. Stinson claims to do, based on the shameful sores of a dead man. Nor can I find guilt there, as Mr. Pearse attempts to do, based solely on her entreaties for forgiveness."

"I find you once again in contempt of court, Miss Hawkins," admonished the judge. "Additional fine of forty shillings imposed. If you continue to defy this court, I shall have you behind bars."

Louise went on. "The attorneys hope that I will answer in a specific fashion, and they become frustrated with me when I do not comply. My lord, Honorable Judge Blair, representing the Crown and this court, places me under oath to tell the truth, then forbids me from doing so, and threatens me with retribution besides, when I attempt to tell the whole of the truth."

Judge Blair, having enough of this cavalier characterization by Louise, became beet red with indignation.

"Miss Hawkins, I sentence you to one day behind bars at the Central Station. If you do not silence yourself at once, I shall double the sentence and have you removed immediately to serve your time."

"Though I cannot read the contents of Anna Perenna's mind," Louise plowed ahead, determined to risk the judge's wrath to get the full truth out, "I can measure dimensions within the room where I found her. I can examine blood still on its walls and floor, and I can stare with unblinking eyes into the wound marking the end of an officer and a husband. I can and have read the autopsy report without blanching. I can be curious about irregularities and inconsistencies in the data, and I can formulate hypotheses to explain them. I can put such hypotheses to tests, and I can vow to accept the outcome of that testing, regardless of my pleasure or distaste at the result."

"Constable," ordered the irate judge, "you will transport the witness to the Central Station and hold her there for forty-eight hours. Miss Hawkins, you will immediately cease this testimony, or I will double the penalties that I have thus far imposed. I will have no person, much less a woman, so flagrantly challenge the authority of this court. You will step down!"

Two constables seized her arms, one on each side, and bore her and her cane to the back of the courtroom. Nevertheless, she persisted. "I know who killed William Perenna, yet no one wishes for you jurymen to hear what I have to say. The judge because I offend him. The prosecutor because he will lose his case. Even Mr. Stinson, obliged to defend Anna Perenna, does not wish you to learn."

"So be it!" Judge Blair roared. "Four days of hard bed and hard food."

Proceeding towards the door with her escorts, she walked backwards, so that she could look on the jury during her exit, and began unwrapping her bandaged left hand.

"William Perenna shot himself," she shouted for all to hear.

The judge shouted for quiet.

"He grasped the barrel of his revolver with his left hand, and he put that barrel to his forehead. He put his right hand around the handle, backwards, and he pulled the trigger with his thumb."

"A week behind bars, Chief Constable! You are to keep Miss Hawkins there a week!" Judge Blair bellowed. "Quiet that woman!" he ordered. The constables dared not.

"I know this to be so," she said, tugging the final strip of gauze from her left hand, "because his hand looked like this!"

She raised her hand in the air. It was covered in dark soot with a burn between the thumb and index finger.

Judge Blair fell silent, along with the entire room. Even her escorts stopped to gawk.

"This is what happens," she projected with unreduced volume, "when one so foolishly, or so despairingly, places a revolver to one's forehead and pulls the trigger. This sooting only happens when one uses a revolver to commit suicide. Combustion gases escape through the gap between cylinder and barrel, coating—even burning—skin held too near."

She looked up at the defendant. The prisoner persisted in her tragic vacancy, but a tear ran down her cheek. Rotating on her good foot, Louise displayed the burn on the web of skin between her left thumb and index finger, ensuring that judge, prisoner, and jury saw proof of Anna Perenna's innocence. "This is from the hot exhaust coming from the muzzle."

She then pointed to the shock of black sooting on the heel of her palm. "This is from the cylinder gap."

She held her hand high so that Anna Perenna could see it, but the prisoner would not look. Louise kept it there nonetheless, to impress the image on the jurymen's minds.

"I do swear," she told them, "while still under my oath to God, that William Perenna's hand looked as mine does, widely sooted, a burn on the web connecting finger and thumb, and concentrated soot on the heel of the palm. I held in my hand the barrel of a Colt Navy revolver as I pressed the muzzle to my forehead, even as I activated the trigger with this thumb."

She raised her left hand, turning it so that the jurors could see both sides. "I held the revolver like this."

With her right hand, she grasped backwards the handle of an imaginary revolver, holding thumb to trigger. With her blistered left hand, she wrapped her fingers around the imaginary barrel. She squeezed the trigger.

"BANG!" she shouted, and let her hands fall. Any revolver she might have been holding would have clattered to the boards in front of her.

"As did Lt. Perenna last week, earlier today I used a Colt 1851 Navy revolver to fire a thirty-six caliber bullet at myself. Unlike him, however, I had no desire to commit suicide. I employed a metal plate before my face, for protection. As you can see, my precaution was not altogether successful."

She allowed the jury and the silent judge to study her broken nose and bruised eyes. Her attempt at levity went unremarked.

"Anna Perenna witnessed her husband shoot and kill himself, believing his death was prompted by her infidelity. But he was troubled by his own infidelity. I suspect she sought his forgiveness before he shot himself, and that she continued to do so, even as I entered. It should make no difference to you jurymen, in any case, why she wished to be forgiven. You now know that she did not murder her husband, and you will never find it in your hearts to vote her guilty, even if you planned to find her *non compos mentis*, even if that *is* her hope. She would allow herself be hanged or sent to an asylum before she would deprive her child of the father's inheritance, which, by law, a child will lose if the father has committed suicide. She would die before she would subject her child to a brutal, heartrending life in a workhouse or an orphanage."

A dreadful silence loomed over the room.

"Mr. Stinson tried his best to save them both," Louise said at last. "But you will see to it that she is neither hanged nor committed to an asylum. There must be a third alternative. A more merciful solution must be found."

She turned and limped at last from the courtroom. The stunned constables tasked with removing her hesitated a beat and then followed her into the street.

Chapter sixteen
A SHOOTING OUTSIDE THE GUILDHALL

Late Monday morning, 24 March 1879
Outside the Guildhall, Broad Street
Bristol, England

Jim Jeffers waited on the steps as Louise exited the Guildhall followed by her tardy, befuddled escorts. Then came the press in a body, a many-footed beast with but one purpose. The reporters tried shouting questions at her, to no avail. Jeffers began to shout louder than the badgering press, and to gesticulate dramatically. "Mr. David Lindsey, owner and editor of the *Bristol North Star,* will now recreate the suicide of William Perenna," Jeffers shouted, "by shooting himself in the forehead with a loaded revolver!"

Events moved quickly after that, so that no one might intervene. As the constables helped Louise into the police van, Lindsey put his back toward the outer wall of the Guildhall, his heels about a foot from it. In his right hand, he held the rented Colt Navy revolver, pointed to the sky, a single cartridge barely visible at the cylinder's ten o'clock position.

Once she was lifted into the prisoner's wagon, Louise seated herself on the bench next to the reporter previously ordered held there. He asked anxiously, "What did I miss?"

Louise leaned towards the barred window next to her, and pointed silently as Lindsey turned the Colt backwards in his left hand, aiming it above his head.

The constables secured the rear door of the van.

Two *North Star* employees held a metal plate in front of Lindsey's face, far enough away that any backward movement would not break his nose. Pasted to the front of the plate was a life-sized photograph of William Perenna's face, complete with gaping bullet wound.

The reporter, Louise's companion, tried desperately to view the proceeding over her shoulder. "What's going on?" he implored. She leaned a bit to her left, allowing the reporter a small view.

"Stand clear," shouted Jeffers, edging people back from the makeshift stage. "No one is to be in the line of fire." He gave his employer the go-ahead.

Lindsey lowered the muzzle to the photograph of William Perenna. With a slow, practiced motion, he grasped the barrel with his left hand and placed the muzzle directly on William Perenna's photographed wound.

Other than a muttered "What the bloody hell?" from the reporter in the police wagon, the audience was absolutely silent. Evidently the wagon driver wanted to see the outcome, so he dallied to observe the spectacle.

Lindsey put his right thumb on the hammer and cocked it, and the loaded chamber rotated into alignment with the barrel. He trembled noticeably as he moved his thumb to the trigger and applied slow, gentle pressure. The hammer dropped. There followed an ear-splitting report, several screams from ladies, and a collective gasp from the crowd, accompanied by an oddly coordinated step backwards.

The bullet flattened itself against the plate, creating a slight indentation in which it stuck. Lindsey allowed the natural recoil of the revolver to free itself from his hands. The weapon landed on pillows placed there for the specific purpose of protecting the rented revolver, as well as Lindsey's fifty-pound surety bond.

Lindsey allowed—almost forced—his feet to slide forward as he fell back, his head hitting and dragging down the wall, landing him in the same awkward position that William Perenna occupied eleven days earlier. He played dead. Blood trickled from his nose.

"Please remain at your distance as we document these results," intoned Jeffers. "We promise to share each and every photograph we make with whatever journalist requests them, and to do so before the *North Star* goes to press."

Spectators, jurymen, attorneys, and even Judge Blair, all lured out onto the Guildhall steps by the report of the gunshot, spilled out and competed with reporters to gain a view.

"Now," shouted Jeffers, "behold Mr. Lindsey's hand!"

In an eerie movement, Lindsey's left hand rose slowly into the air, while the rest of Lindsey remained deceased. The appendage was badly burned and covered with soot. Jeffers held a photograph of William Perenna's soot-smudged left hand beside Lindsey's. "This is a photograph of Lt. Perenna's hand," Jeffers explained. The distinctive smudge on the palm heel and the burning of the thumb webbing—both matched. After the spectators had enough time to compare the two hands, Lindsey's raised limb rejoined the rest of his corpse on the ground.

Jeffers laid the photograph next to Lindsey's hand, then set up his camera to document the matching patterns, explaining all the while Lindsey's demonstration. He took silent notice of his employer's slight, pained grimace, despite his valiant effort to be a corpse for the camera. Lindsey had anticipated the burn; he had placed his hand as far from the muzzle as the weapon's dimensions would allow, but the resulting injury nonetheless approached the severity of Louise's.

Jeffers checked his pocket watch. "Be patient with us for just a few seconds more, gentlemen. Then we shall have a doctor tend you, Mr. Lindsey," he said loudly enough that all could hear. "Good show, sir. I daresay, one of the most stunning I have ever seen."

Lindsey declined to take a bow. He gamely maintained his morbid pose.

The demonstration complete, the driver of the Black Maria shook the reins to urge the horses forward. Louise sat back with a sigh. The reporter pressed his face to the bars of the window and yelled, "See that the *Morning Mail* gets a copy!"

As the wagon left the square abutting the Guildhall, Louise observed, through the back window, the judge, the court officials, the spectators, and the jurymen filing back inside, chatting with animation about the entertainment they'd just seen, visibly disappointed that they had another trial to sit through.

She closed her aching eyes and sat silently as the Black Maria conveyed her to jail.

chapter seventeen
VERDICT AND PUNISHMENT

Monday afternoon, 24 March 1879
The Guildhall, Broad Street
Bristol, England

After a lively session in the jury chambers, the jury for the Court of Assizes returned verdicts on the seven cases it had heard that day.

The jury found John Skelton guilty of stealing the boots of John Hinson. Judge Blair sentenced Skelton to twelve months' hard labor.

They found William Roult guilty of breaking into the dwelling house of Robert Nicholls and stealing various articles, for which he also received twelve months hard labor.

Charles Bird and Thomas Groves were found guilty of sending diseased meat to the London market. Judge Blair sentenced Bird and Groves to three months' hard labor.

Eleven-year-old Sallie Mills Alden was found guilty of picking six shillings from a lady's handbag. The judge sentenced her to one month of jail time at the Central Station and eleven months in the Red Lodge Girl's Reformatory School. He told her sternly that it was a much lighter sentence than she might have received.

The jury determined that Edward Deacon murdered his wife. Covering his white wig with a black cloth, Judge Blair sentenced Deacon to hang by his neck until dead.

In the audience sat a man with a dent just above his right temple. With the last verdict, he began to mumble quietly, barely overheard even by those sitting close to him. "Please, dear God. No more, no more. I can't do it. I won't do it."

After a long, fraught pause, the jury announced their determination that Anna Perenna was not guilty of murdering her husband. Judge Blair told her that she was free to go. A constable escorted her from the dock and released her to Jim Jeffers, the person appointed by Lindsey to see her safely home. Jeffers wrapped her in a gray hooded cloak and guided her out the back entrance, where they entered a waiting brougham carriage driven by a fellow in a black cloak tipped at the collar with red.

Inside the Guildhall, John Fellows was found guilty of fowl stealing. In large measure because of his many previous offenses, Judge Blair sentenced him to seven years' hard labor.

But the judge was not quite done. After quashing Quinton Welsh's indictment against Anna Perenna, the first of Mr. Welsh's indictments ever to be quashed, Judge Blair ruled that any subsequent inquest would be impossible, since no future proceeding could be held in the presence of an already buried body. The heavy burden of ruling on Lt. Perenna's manner of death, Judge Blair declared, with patently false unwillingness, unfortunately fell upon him. It was therefore with great reluctance, he claimed, that he found Lt. Perenna to have died of suicide.

"Self-murder," the judge explained, patiently, "is wisely and religiously considered by the English law as the most heinous variety of felonious homicide; for, as no man has the right to destroy life, but by commission of God, the author of all life, he who commits suicide is guilty of a double offense: one spiritual, in evading the prerogative of the Almighty, and the other against the Queen, who has an interest in the preservation of all her subjects. Lt. Perenna's offense, therefore, is a *felo de se*, a felony committed on oneself.

"What punishment apportioned to the enormity of the offense can human laws impose upon one who has withdrawn himself from their reach? Upon his body they are inoperative; they can only act upon that which he has left behind, his fortune and his reputation. Since one of the great objects of punishment is example, the forfeiture of property and the imposition of an ignominious burial will deter others from sacrificing the welfare of their family, and their reputation, by so wicked and desperate an act. The law is clear on this point, and this court has no latitude in its verdict. This court commands that all of Lt. William Perenna's money, property, and chattels are hereby forfeited to the Crown. This court commands further that the body of Lt. Perenna be exhumed and reburied within the walls of New Jail Prison."

MONDAY EVENING, 24 MARCH 1879
22 TORQUAY TERRACE
CLIFTON, ENGLAND

To shield herself from the reporters outside, Anna Perenna closed the curtains at the house on Torquay Terrace. As the reporters banged on the door and tapped at the windows, she tried to scrub her husband's blood and brains from the wall and floor of the home that, until Judge Blair's ruling a few hours earlier, had been hers. Her plan to keep secret the suicide had failed. The natural consequences were soon to follow.

She felt the baby kick and turn. She sat on the floor and rubbed her belly, trying to comfort her child and herself, but thinking of the bleak future in store for both of them.

The widow Perenna had no money, no possessions, no skills or education to speak of. She had never held a meaningful job. All she had was a publicly declared act of adultery, a sullied reputation, and a baby who would soon be demanding far more than she could provide, one certain to never have prospects for a good marriage or a good life, being a bastard. Anna could turn to prostitution, but her prospects, living on the streets, were bleak. She would leave her baby at the door of an orphanage before she turned to whatever new life awaited. At least that way the child might escape the stigma of being born to such a mother.

It would have worked out, she thought, had that Hawkins woman not seen through the ploy. The baby would have its father's home and pension, and those assets would perhaps have encouraged adoption by some family of means.

Had she been found *non compos mentis*, she might have actually met the grown child someday. That was always unlikely though. More probable that she would have been hanged soon after giving birth. Even that would have been better for the child than the long agony ahead.

She gently massaged the contours of her beloved passenger. "Please forgive me," she said, softly. "Please, dear child, forgive me."

TUESDAY, 25 MARCH 1879
BRISTOL POLICE CENTRAL STATION, BRIDEWELL STREET
BRISTOL, ENGLAND

The day after the trial, the newspapers led with the story of an obviously innocent woman, pregnant no less, nearly hanged due to the incompetence and prejudice of everyone other than high-minded reporters and editors. Though the Jezebel deserved all the scorn heaped upon her, they wrote, even she did not deserve to hang for a crime she did not commit.

Each and every one of the newspapers included the photograph comparing the gunpowder patterns on the hands of David Lindsey and William Perenna.

Most of the weeklies rushed out special editions, the *Bristol North Star* among them. As per their agreement, David Lindsey downplayed Louise's role in the case, and no one ever learned of Jeremy's involvement.

Judge Blair modified the contempt penalty imposed on Louise to time already served. Detective John Reeves, eager to inform her that she was free, was surprised when she insisted on serving the entire seven-day sentence. He hesitantly asked if she would mind him calling on her, once matters settled, but she did not respond. He reproached himself for such an untimely and selfish intrusion, and vowed to never again disturb her, to spend his time instead searching for the man with the dent in his forehead.

Upon learning of Louise's lack of appreciation for his mercy, Judge Blair declared her in trespass of Crown property and ordered that she be removed, with force if necessary. Three jailers tried, but she thrust her arms between the bars and interlocked her fingers. As the two men pulled Louise from behind, the matron attempted to pry apart Louise's fingers, but stopped in horror at the snap of a knuckle and a scream of pain.

Dr. Daniel Weston arrived within the hour. After removing his silk-lined bowler and installing his pince-nez spectacles upon the bridge of his nose, he examined Louise's injuries. He set the obviously dislocated small finger of her right hand, splinting it and taping it to the two adjoining fingers. He applied an ointment to the burns on her left hand, and then rebandaged it. He told her that her ankle was healing more slowly than expected, that she might have broken a bone, and he wrapped the ankle tightly for her, advising that her foot should be in a cast and that she should keep off it as much as possible.

Her nose was definitely broken and must soon be set, he said, lest it be deformed forever. Informing her that the procedure would be quick but painful, he offered several doses of laudanum, which she accepted. Despite the sedative and her resolution to be stoic, she screamed for a second time when the doctor put his hands on either side of her nose and snapped it left, then right, to reset the bone and cartilage.

"It will be nearly perfect when it heals," he told her. He suspected the renewed bruises around her eyes would be spectacular for several weeks.

He gathered his miscellaneous tools and supplies, walked to the cell door, which the jailers had taken to leaving open, then turned for a last look and a last word.

"Thank you," he said, "for keeping me from being involved in the execution of an innocent person."

———⁂———

WEDNESDAY, 26 MARCH 1879
BRISTOL POLICE CENTRAL STATION, BRIDEWELL STREET
BRISTOL, ENGLAND

Other than Dr. Weston, Louise refused to take any visitors.
Mrs. Croton arrived early with a basket of meat pies, an ap-
ple crumble, and a bottle of wine. She was reluctantly turned
away by jailers whose mouths watered for the old widow's
offerings.

In the afternoon, David Lindsey arrived with news of the
day. He vowed to visit daily in hopes that she would see him,
but he would be rejected each time. The jailers relayed a message that he would be the first to receive a call from her after
her seven days expired.

She occupied the long hours sitting quietly on the splintery
bench, trying to understand the blurry distinctions between
right and wrong, trying to distinguish fact from desire. She
pondered the vagaries of life and thought of William Perenna's
fall from grace, the exhumation of his body, and his reburial
within prison walls.

What did it matter where you lay, she thought, once you
were dead? In a dirty prison or a marble tower on top of a
high hill? You were dead, you were sleeping the long sleep that
awaits us all. You were not bothered by trifles such as scenery.
Soil and water were the same to you as wind and air. You just
slept the long sleep, not caring about the nastiness of how you
died, or where you fell, or where you lay.

Her thoughts turned, as they frequently did, to her aged
father, sixty-three years her senior, lying quietly in his bed,
his bloodless hand in hers, his breaths coming infrequently,
in soft bursts, his thoughts as gray as ashes. The pain and ter-
ror were finally in the past. And Louise had known, as she sat
beside him six years earlier, that he would soon embark on
his long sleep, and that subsequently their shared memories
would be hers alone.

chapter eighteen

MRS. ANNA HEBRON

On the fifth day of Louise's self-prolonged incarceration, Anna Perenna, escorted by David Lindsey, arrived and asked for a visit. Louise agreed to meet with Anna, and just Anna.

Considerably less disheveled than Louise remembered her, but even more pregnant, which had not seemed possible, Anna appeared in the always-open cell doorway. Louise sat quietly on the bench, and each of them took the measure of the other. Louise then patted the bench to her right. Anna waddled over and laboriously lowered herself, one hand braced on the wall behind her, the other cradling her immense belly.

For two long minutes, the two sat side-by-side, neither saying a word, neither looking at the other. Except for the normal jailhouse sounds beyond the cell, their silence was interrupted only twice, each time by a deep sigh issued from Anna, each sigh prompted by another failure on her part to bring herself to speak. She succeeded, finally, on her third try.

"I hated you," she said, her stare still forward, "for what you did."

Louise nodded, lips pursed.

"For the dismal future that you would inflict on my child." She caressed her swollen belly, then collapsed into tears.

Louise embraced the broken woman and held her, just as she had during that horrible morning on Torquay Terrace.

"Forgive me," Anna sobbed. "Please forgive me."

"There's nothing to forgive," said Louise, holding her even closer, softly rocking with her. "You were willing to sacrifice everything for your child, even your life. Such courage, such nobility, such love demands not forgiveness but respect."

Anna wrapped her arms around Louise and whimpered into her shoulder, "Forgive me for hating you."

"I'll forgive you, Anna Perenna," said Louise, tears suddenly prickling at her own eyes, her long-suppressed emotions finally getting the better of her, "if you will forgive me for being the cause of the hardships that await you and your child."

The two sat there for many minutes, in each other's arms, Anna crying on Louise's shoulder, Louise occasionally wiping away her own tears with the sleeve of her jail-soiled dress.

"I so look forward to a bath and a change of clothes," Louise finally said, breaking the tension and prompting a bit of lightness from Anna.

They separated, looked each other in the eye, and wiped the wetness from the other's cheeks.

"I've had time to think," said Louise. "I would like to introduce you to my mother. She has seven children so far, but no grandchildren yet, nor likely any in the foreseeable future. I suspect she would be pleased to add another daughter to her brood, particularly if that daughter gave her a grandchild to love."

Anna looked away. Without responding to Louise's offer, she finally said, "Mr. and Mrs. Lindsey have taken me in."

She paused, deciding carefully her next words.

"They are both so wonderful." She took a breath. "I can't find words to express my appreciation. I doubt I'll ever be able to do so."

Louise produced an encouraging smile.

"And Mr. Lindsey has offered me a position as a apprentice typesetter," Anna added, suddenly, her words and dreams and aspirations coming in a torrent. "He said that if I work hard and excel and save, I will be able to afford a place of my own before too long. It would be small, no doubt, and maybe a bit shabby at first, at least until I could clean and fix it to my satisfaction, but it would be wonderful for just the baby and me. And you could visit, and I'd serve tea and biscuits!"

"That will indeed be wonderful," replied Louise. "But you avoided responding to my offer. Even with the Lindseys being so marvelously helpful, I would still like you to meet my mother, and I still would like to think of you as a sister. It would be marvelous to regard your child as a niece or nephew."

Anna looked away, then down, but not so quickly as to conceal the sadness and worry written on her face. She sighed to build her courage, then, sight still fixed at the dirty floor, began her story.

"I've told no one, not even Mr. or Mrs. Lindsey, of what happened. I will tell you though, and you may then decide if you would indeed like me as your sister, and my child as your niece or nephew."

She took another long breath.

"My parents died when I was young. The only childhood I knew was the orphanage and the workhouse, and I'd not wish that on any child, particularly not one of my own. I eventually found menial work in a tannery, saved what money I could, and at long last set out for America, to begin a new and better life. In Atlanta, I met, fell in love with, and married a man named John Hebron. He was smart and kind and passionate, and my life was nothing less than a miracle, but only for a little while. With no warning whatsoever, the police broke down our door and hauled him off to jail. Their only explanation was that our marriage was illegal. I tried to visit him in jail, then later in prison, but they denied me, always with the same explanation. Our marriage was invalid, they would say, and I was therefore not kin, with no right to visit him. Some said, since I had not been his wife, that I was his whore."

She paused. Louise waited patiently. Anna straightened, easing against the wall with a hand to the small of her back.

"Then, after five months of his imprisonment and hard labor in the swamps, I received word that he had succumbed to a particularly deadly strain of malaria. Even dead—"

Another deep breath.

"—the prison officials refused to let me see him. I decided, then and there, to forever abandon my new world of despair for my native land of misery. Better the devil you know, as they say."

She wiped a single tear from her cheek.

"What could I do? I found myself working once again in a tannery, this time in Redcliff, not far from here. I was miserable, and that suited me. The world had taken John from me, and I intended to repay it by never again experiencing a moment of happiness. Then I met William. For him, I felt just a touch of what I had before. He was not as bright or passionate as John, but he had a brutishness about him that somehow appealed to me. I believed I deserved nothing better.

"For a brief while, he served as a good enough husband and provider. We began to build a life. It was occasionally pleasant, though far from perfect, our years in that little house. We promised each other to go out at least once each week, to the zoological gardens, or to the observatory, or simply to a park with a basket lunch, perhaps someday even to Leigh Court to view the masterpieces. For another short time, I was content enough, thinking that I would pass my remaining days in such circumstance. But it was not to be.

"Last March, William's unit was sent to Afghanistan. Oh, but I soldiered on, just as he did. I put as much spit and polish to our little home as I could. I wrote to him frequently. Only a single letter in reply ever came.

"One day July last, I received shocking news. A messenger arrived to inform me that my beloved John was alive, and in England, but deathly ill with cholera. I rushed to him in his dirty little room by the quay. The story was just as marvelous as I had been told: he was indeed alive. And it was just as terrible as I feared: he was in deadly peril from his ailment.

"I embraced him, kissed him, and bathed him, all the while voicing my love for him. I felt my hopes for our future rekindled. When he felt well enough, I had relations with him."

She paused her narrative and turned to Louise to ensure that she had been understood. Louise nodded, and Anna returned her gaze to the wall opposite.

"Obviously, he had not died while in prison. He had indeed suffered greatly from malaria, however, and his kidneys had been badly damaged. His body would be forevermore vulnerable to infection and disease. The prison officials, he explained, had lied to me about his death so I would stop pestering them. Worse, far worse, they told him what they had done, laughing at their devious deception as he raged at their cruelty.

"When he was finally freed, he tracked me all the way to Bristol. The search had not been difficult, since I had retained his name, Hebron. He learned that I had married again. With no wish to unnecessarily complicate my life, he merely watched me from afar. I seemed content, so he decided to return to America and leave me to my new life.

"Just then, though, William was sent to Afghanistan. John learned of this and could not bring himself to leave. Still he hid from me, watching as I hung laundry, or planted vegetables, or walked to the market, all the while longing to talk to me, to touch me, to hold me, to love me. But he resisted."

Anna sighed.

"When struck with the cholera, he knew it would be the end of him, so weak were his kidneys. He could resist his love no longer. He yearned to see me one last time, to tell me that he loved me, that he always had, and always would."

She wiped at a tear. Another fell, without interruption, onto her bodice, and she broke down, sobbing with the mortal despair of her memories. After several minutes she quieted.

"He died the next day, in my arms. I wonder every day if being with me once more caused the relapse that carried him away."

She drew a large silver locket from her bosom. She touched a spring, and the front hinged back. She handed the locket to Louise. There was a portrait within of a man, strikingly handsome and intelligent, bearing unmistakable signs upon his features of his African descent.

"That is John Hebron, of Atlanta," said Anna, "and a nobler man never walked the earth."

Louise smiled gently, nodded, and returned the locket. Anna closed it and returned it to her bosom.

"When William returned, after a year in Afghanistan, I was eight months with child. He was furious. I tried to tell him of my prior marriage, of how I had been deceived as to my first husband's death, of John's miraculous reappearance, and what I refer to as his second death. But I could hardly relate John's story, so enraged was William. I had never seen him so angry before, and I was admittedly terrified, both for myself and the baby. He took off his boots and removed his trousers, right there in the front room, and demanded his nuptial rights. He used the coarsest of terms, making clear that if I did not provide them willingly, he would claim them by force."

She took one long breath, then another, before continuing.

"I noticed the sore on his member, the mere mention of which at trial caused such stir, and I feared even more for my child. I pleaded with him. When he began to tear at my clothing and pull me to the bedroom, I appealed to him not to lie on me or the baby. So he took me from behind, like the base animal that he is. He granted me this indignity as if it were a blessing.

"When the act was done, he told me he would leave the house for an hour, and when he returned I should be gone. I was no longer his wife, he said, and had in fact never been so, already married that I was. Never mind that he'd demanded *his rights* as a husband moments before. He asked me what he should tell his mates such that they would not scorn or mock him, but I had no answer. He stormed out to dress, afterwards to leave me alone yet again."

"I cleansed myself twice, with carbolic then with vinegar. I donned my other dress and arranged my hair as best I could. I turned on the stove and set a teapot. I walked to the living room to bid William farewell, not caring a whit what would become of me, wondering only how I could maintain myself until my baby was born."

She put her hands to her face, palms on cheeks, fingers pressed over closed eyes. Louise sat beside her, with a breaking heart.

"He was waiting for me when I entered, with his back to the wall, and dressed, save his boots, still where he had dropped them. He held his revolver in one hand and my locket open in the other. It must have fallen to the floor as we struggled, and he noticed it as he dressed. I will not repeat the filthy words he spewed as he raged about telling his mates he had been cuckolded by such a man as John Hebron. I was hard put to reason why he should tell his mates anything. How our thoughts can stray in the midst of such an incredible mess!

"He tossed the locket at me, and I caught it and held it to my bosom. I knew he was going to shoot me, that I had but moments to live. I was determined to spend those few moments with my one true love as close to my heart as possible. I stepped towards William, defiant and proud, no longer wanting to live, no longer afraid to die. 'Shoot me!' I said. I said it quietly at first, then I said it more loudly."

The vision of the trauma overwhelmed her. Louise edged closer on the bench and again wrapped an arm around the suffering woman.

"I can't, " said Anna. "You'll hate me if I tell you what I did."

"I could never hate you, Anna Hebron. You and I have a bond that can never be broken."

A long pause, agonizing in its tension, ensued.

"I killed him," Anna said.

Louise tensed.

"I killed him," Anna repeated. "Not by shooting him. That was all just as you said. No, I didn't kill William with his gun. I didn't need to. I used words. I didn't shoot him, but I killed him just as surely as though I had, by saying—no, by screaming—'Shoot me! Shoot me, if you're man enough!'

"He pointed the gun at me for so long, I nearly fainted with anxiety. And then he turned it in his hands and seized its barrel so quickly! I didn't even have a chance to cry out. His face was so twisted and ugly. And he—he—"

Anna buried her face in Louise's dress and cried.

chapter nineteen

NEW BIRTH, NEW LIFE

For all her shortcomings, Louise thought, *Mrs. Croton serves a lovely cup of tea.* Louise was sipping the widow's tea from the widow's china, sitting in the widow's bay window, her casted leg on the widow's ottoman. She watched young couples stroll in the park. She wondered if Detective Reeves might call on her, hoping that he would, expecting that he would not. It was the sort of peaceful moment that Louise had welcomed in the weeks since the conclusion of the Perenna affair, the harrowing but inspiring time she knew had changed her forever. Blood, bodies, and brimstone—the stuff of mankind's greatest stories, as well as its most horrific ones, which she realized were really just two ways of phrasing the same thought.

Of late, she had been considering the newspapers' salacious reporting of Anna Perenna's ordeal, from her husband's suicide to Anna's ultimate vindication—such as it was—in Judge Blair's courtroom. No one had yet told the entirety of the story. None, save Anna or Louise herself, could. Doing so, however, would surely make total the shame and regret felt by the young mother-to-be.

Is not such love between two souls a pure and good thing worthy of praise, Louise mused, no matter the bloodlines thus entwined? And for that fact alone, would it not be worthwhile to find an audience to hear of the bond that drew together Anna and the man whose portrait graced her locket? The bond that first united them in America, then returned them to each other's arms after cruel hearts tore them apart?

She sighed.

No, the public would not accept it. John Hebron had been a sable son of Africa. Though his ancestral homeland was, according to Darwin, the ancestral homeland of us all, too many eyes and too many hearts remain blind to the traits that unite us.

She regretted that she would not live long enough to see much fundamental change in people, though machines and devices somehow continue to progress at ever faster speeds. Rearranging molecules is child's play, she realized, compared to altering cherished beliefs, particularly those long passed from one imperfect generation to the next. Mankind, she concluded, is a puzzle wrapped in a conundrum swaddled in an enigma, capable of magnificent achievements and horrific acts, even those that lie far beyond our wildest imaginings.

A young and energetic messenger just then interrupted her thoughts by riding his Ariel bicycle at reckless speed up the street, somehow hopping the curb without damaging either tire, and stopping abruptly, just short of Mrs. Croton's front steps. He leapt from the cycle, rushed up the steps, and thrashed the bell.

"I'm coming, I'm coming," yelled Mrs. Croton, as she pattered her way from the kitchen to the foyer.

"Telegram for Miss Louise Hawkins," announced the lad, with sufficient volume for all to hear.

There was a noticeable lag between the brief discussion at the door and Mrs. Croton's arrival at Louise's side.

"It's for you," the landlady sang. "No telling who might have sent it."

Louise noted that the telegram was already unsealed. As she read to herself, her landlady pretended to fuss over a snag in one of the lace curtains.

MORNING BIRTH. HEALTHY BOY. ANNA SAFE AND RESTING. SHE NAMED HIM DAVID JEREMIAH HEBRON. AM HUMBLED. CALL WHEN POSSIBLE. LINDSEY.

Louise smiled.

"It's good news, then?" ventured Mrs. Croton, having abruptly lost interest in the curtain. Louise stood and mounted her crutch with practiced grace, found her gloves, and slipped into her jacket. "I'm afraid I cannot stay to finish your delightful Darjeeling. I must hop out."

The landlady blinked, visibly disappointed at being deprived of gossip. "But—"

"I've no time," said Louise, pinning her hat in place. "The shops will soon close for business, and I must find a suitable gift for a baby boy."

"Baby boy? Whose?" Mrs. Croton practically cried with desperation.

Before looking up, Louise ensured, with a glance and a swift shuffle of contents, that her purse held a sufficiency of coins.

"My sister's," Louise said, beaming, making her way to the door.

author's note

The story that you have read is a work of fiction, or approximately so. In my nonfiction book *Shadow Woman: The Real Creator of Sherlock Holmes*, I provide compelling evidence that Sherlock Holmes was created not by the famous Arthur Conan Doyle, but rather by his first wife, Louise, a version of whom you have just met. Generally ignored, dismissed, and disparaged by Arthur's many biographers, Louise was in reality a kind, generous, and brilliant woman. We know little of her today because the documents that preserved her history were destroyed by Arthur's second wife and family.

Georgina Doyle, the wife of Arthur's nephew, began revealing Louise's story in *Out of The Shadows: The Untold Story of Arthur Conan Doyle's First Family* (2004). Even Ms. Doyle, though, failed to discover the whole truth. In *Shadow Woman*, I continue Louise's rehabilitation and reveal, for the first time, how Sherlock Holmes was born of Louise's mind and pen.

In this series, I add color to her narrative by having her solve one baffling mystery after another, both before and after she meets Arthur, even as she writes the early Holmes adventures. Some details are based on fact, others on surmise.

Brimstone is a novel, but its premise is, tragically, the stuff of real life.

An ocean away, and more than a century after the events depicted in this book, in the predawn hours of 23 October 1997, a night-patrol deputy discovered the body of Anastasia WitbolsFeugen lying across the narrow road that runs through Missouri's Lincoln Cemetery, near Kansas City. The eighteen-year-old was dead of a contact gunshot wound to the nose.

Four and a half years later, a jury found Byron Case guilty of murdering her, based on the suborned perjury of his embittered ex-girlfriend, Kelly Moffett. Contrary to her earlier assertions of having no knowledge of the shooting, Ms. Moffett suddenly claimed that she witnessed Mr. Case shoot Ms. WitbolsFeugen, their friend, from behind, from a distance of five feet, with a shotgun, or perhaps a rifle. Mr. Case insisted that he was innocent. The judge sentenced him to life imprisonment without the possibility of parole.

Supporters of Byron Case later obtained copies of autopsy photographs that were withheld from Mr. Case and his defense counsel. In those images, Ms. WitbolsFeugen's hands are covered in telltale residue patterns—a textbook example of someone holding the barrel of a black powder revolver as it is fired.

Just as Louise and Lindsey did (or did not do) a century ago, I searched for a likely copy of the weapon used in the shooting, testing several, with unsatisfactory results, until I settled on a readily available replica of an 19th century Colt .36 caliber, snub nose, black powder revolver. With that weapon I was able to recreate the residue patterns found on the hands and face of Anastasia WitbolsFeugen, not by firing at myself (since that would be incredibly stupid), but instead using specially designed targets and wooden artist's hands.

I have shared my revealing and exculpatory test results, during personal visits, with staff of the Missouri Governor, Eric Greitens, and the Jackson County Prosecutor, Jean Peters Baker. I continue to work with those officers to help them understand how Anastasia WitbolsFeugen came to be shot, and how Byron Case came to be convicted for a crime he did not commit.

As of this writing, Byron Case remains locked away in the maximum-security Crossroads Correctional Center in Cameron, Missouri, his life taken from him by a justice system that chose to suborn perjury and to suppress evidence rather than understand its significance.

To learn more about Louise Conan Doyle or Sherlock Holmes, visit *www.louiseconandoyle.com.*

If you are interested in learning more about Byron Case or wrongful convictions, view the blog at *www.skepticaljuror.com.*

And prepare yourself for *Gambit*, the second book in the Louise Conan Doyle Mystery Series. In *Gambit*, Louise finds herself reluctantly drawn into the case of a condemned man scheduled for hanging within days. When you find yourself in the midst of *Gambit*, assume nothing to be true. Trust no one.